My name is
I am years old.
My teacher's name is
AF584375

Track the letters when you have completed the matching pages in your work book. Join the letters to the picture that starts with that letter. Colour the picture.

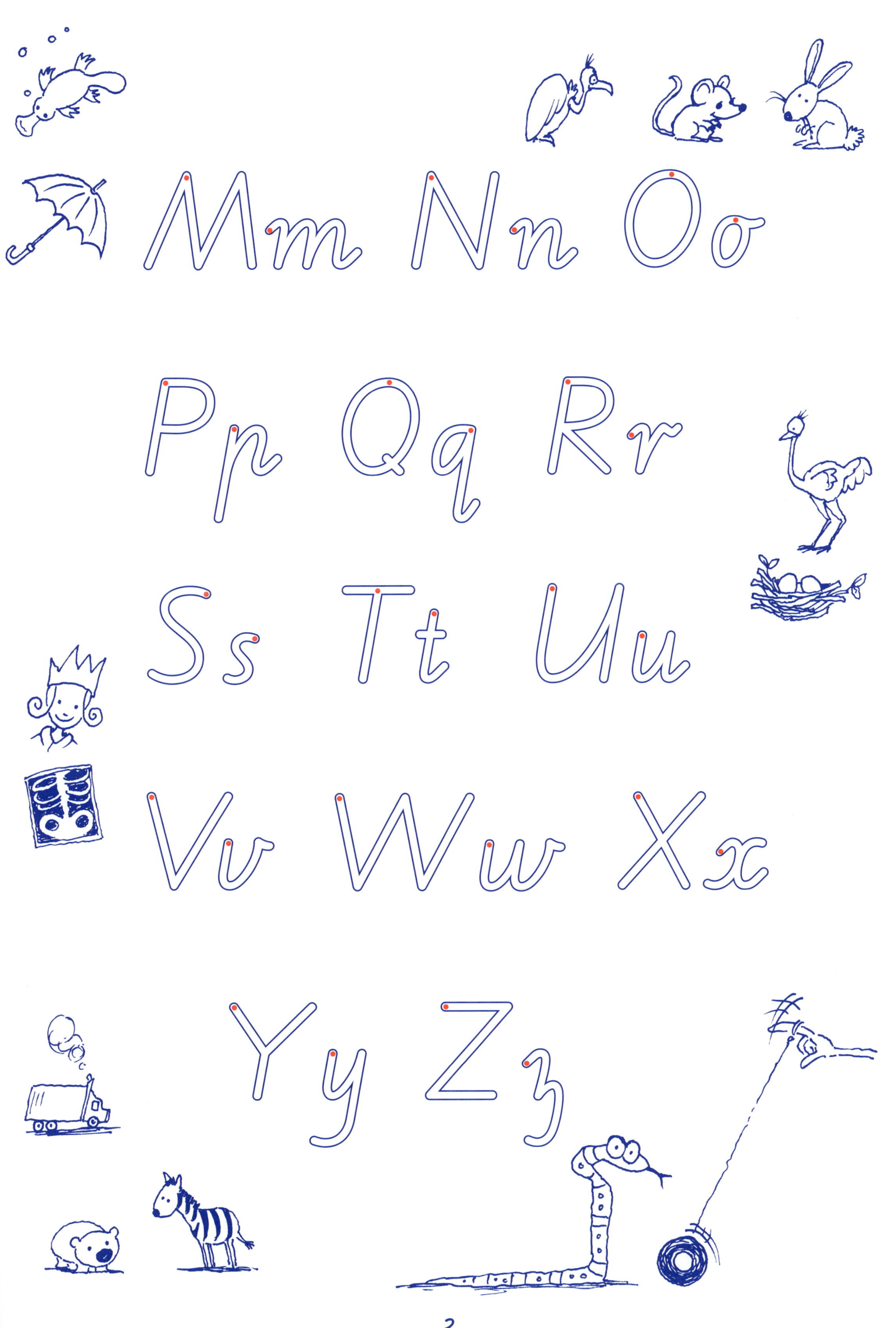

Mm Nn Oo
Pp Qq Rr
Ss Tt Uu
Vv Ww Xx
Yy Zz

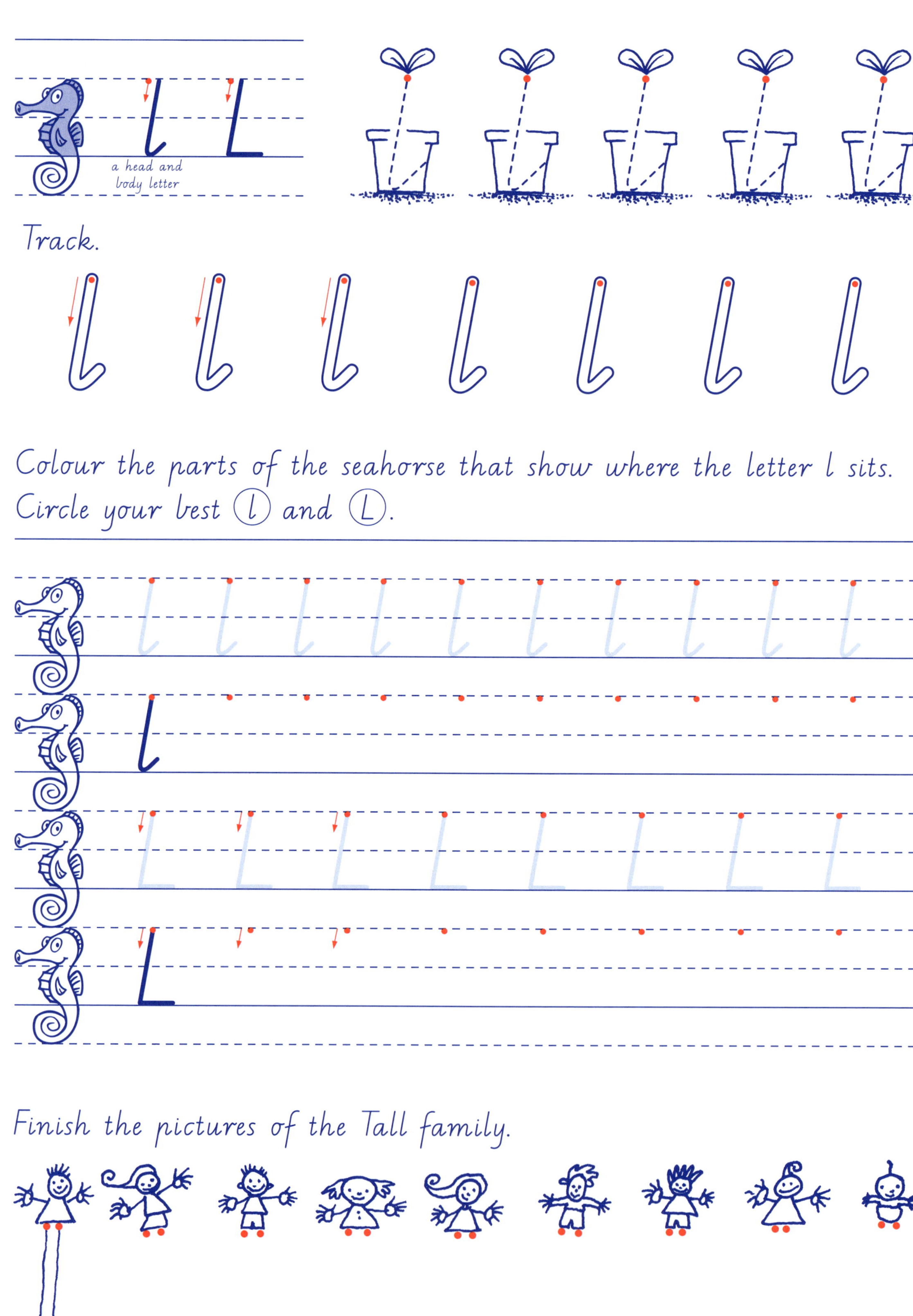

Track.

Colour the parts of the seahorse that show where the letter l sits.
Circle your best (l) and (L).

Finish the pictures of the Tall family.

Find the l's.

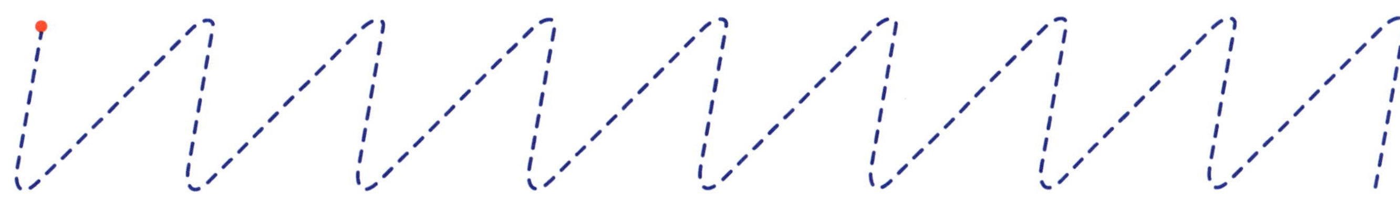

Trace these letters from the i family.

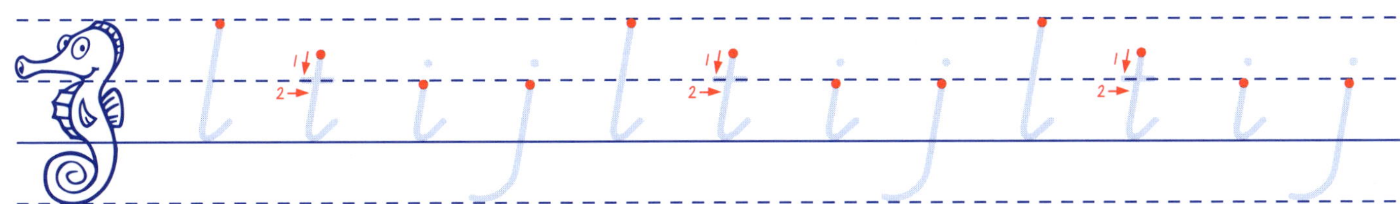

Trace, then copy.

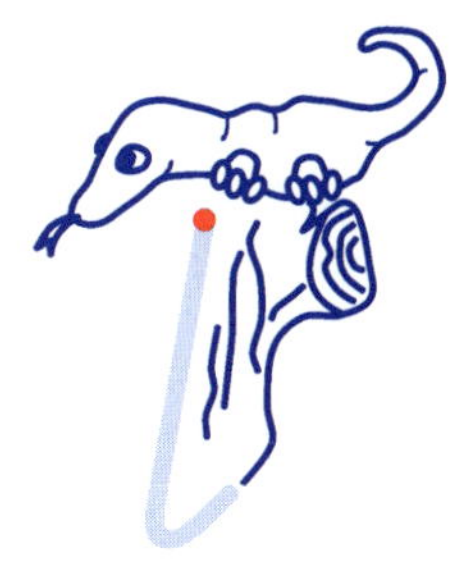
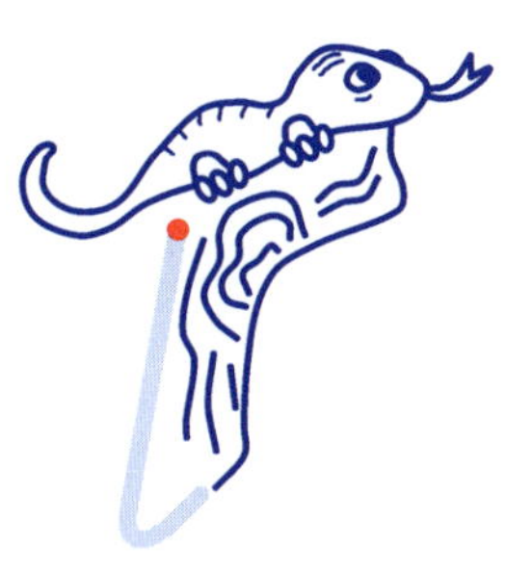
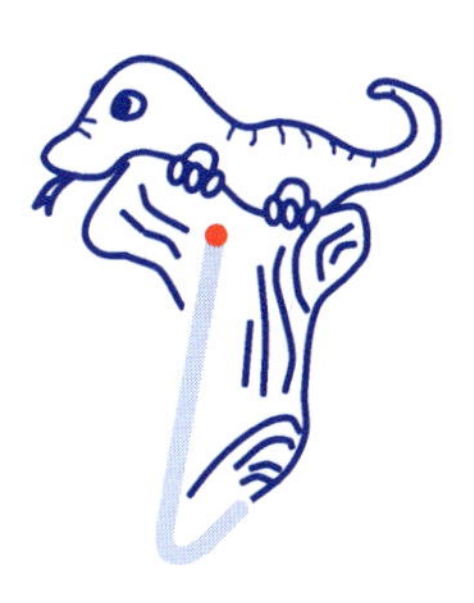
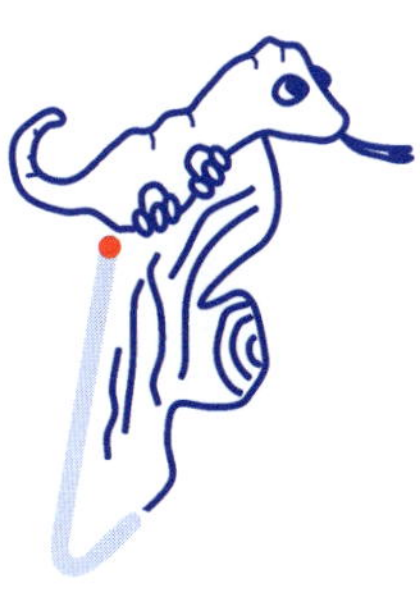

t T
a head and body letter
Track.
Colour the parts of the seahorse that show where the letter t sits.
Place a ✓ on your best t and T.
Left-handers
Finish the road train.
Tate's
Ca
ttle

Find the t's in the saw.

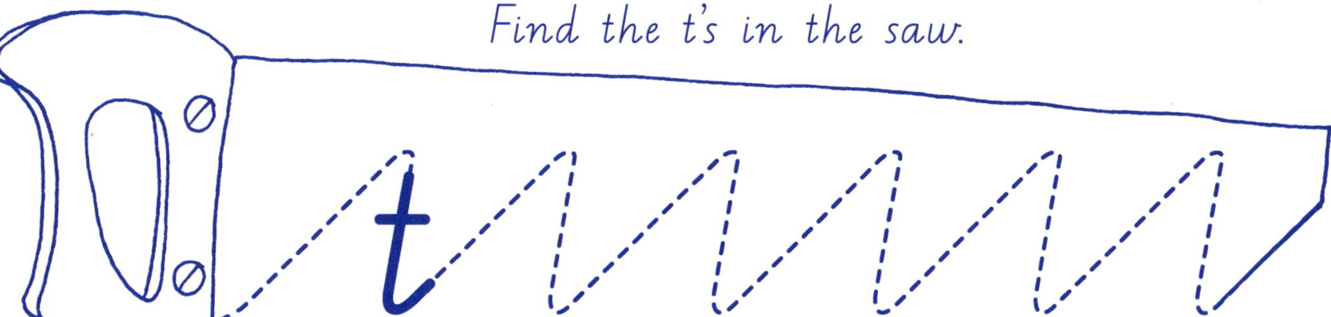

Trace the head and body letters.

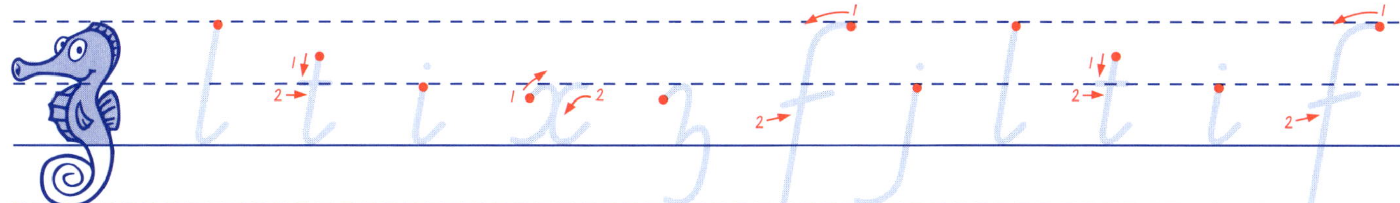

Trace, then copy. Don't forget to draw the seahorses.

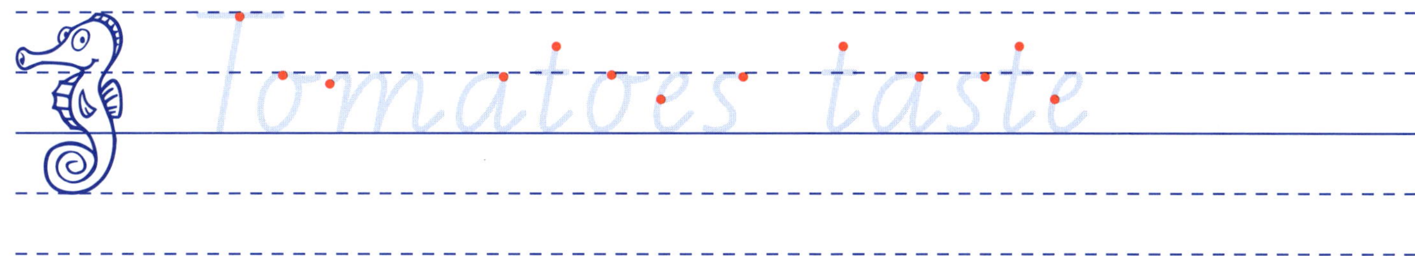

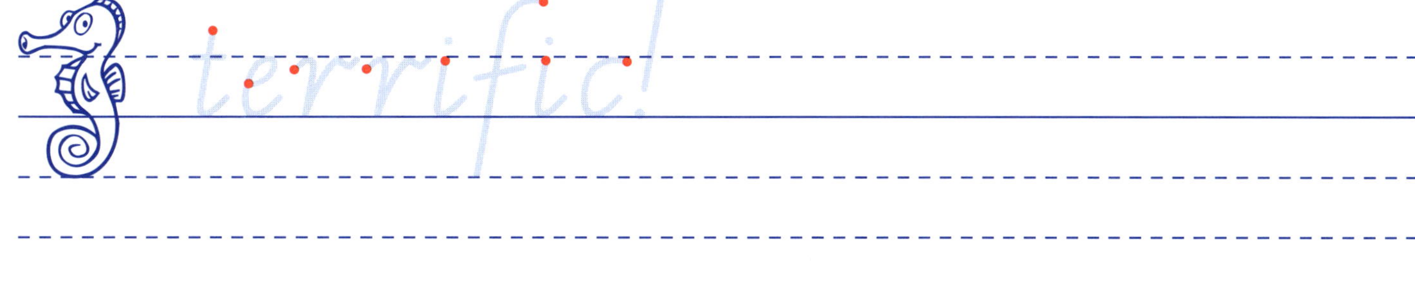

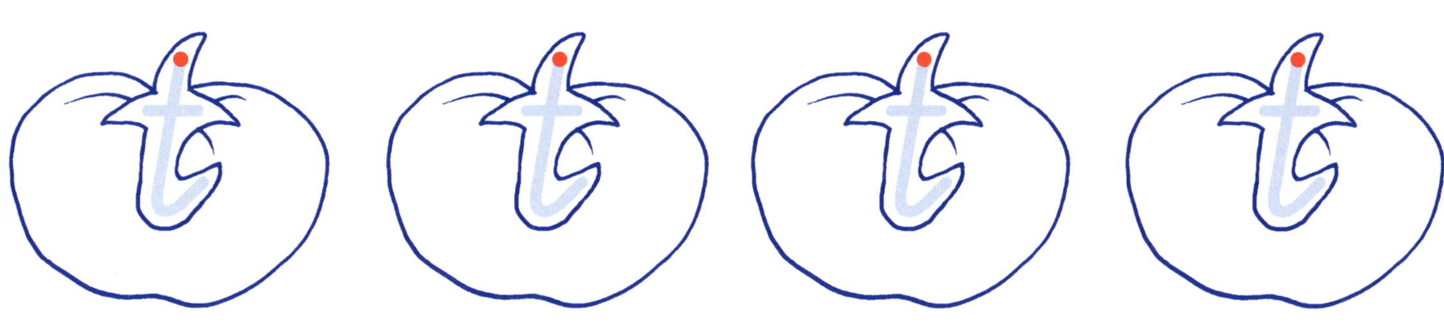

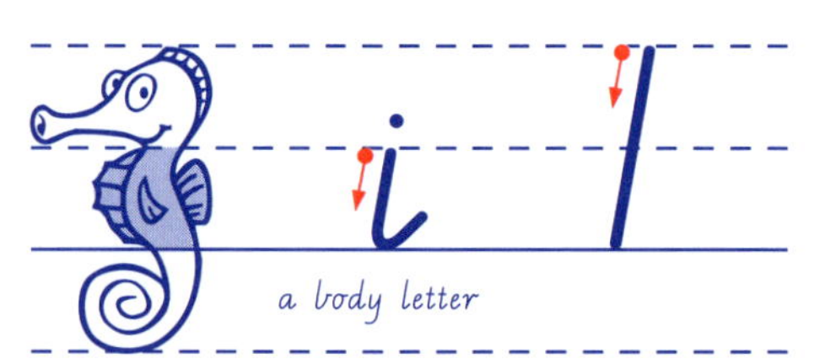

Track.

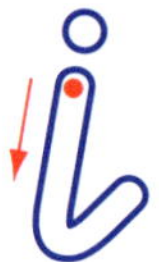      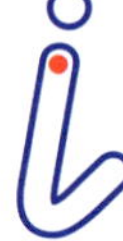

Colour the parts of the seahorse that show where the letter i sits.
Put an X under your best i and l.

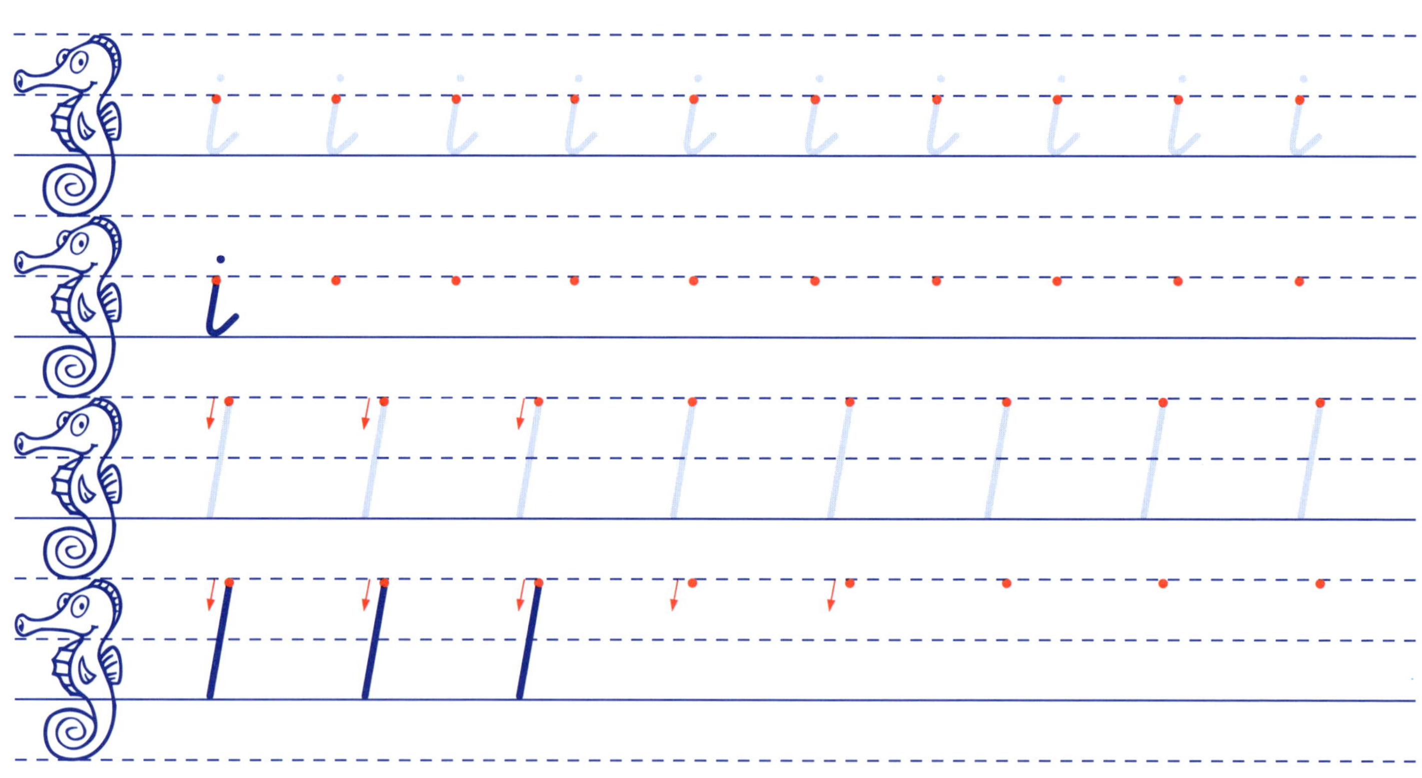

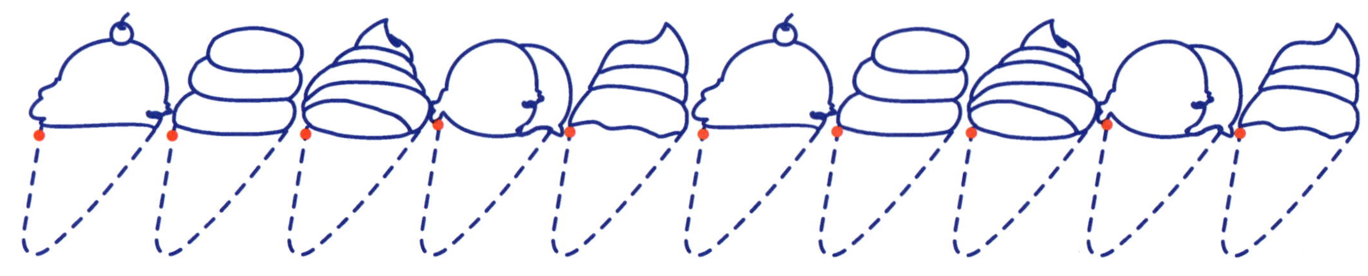

Trace the body letters.

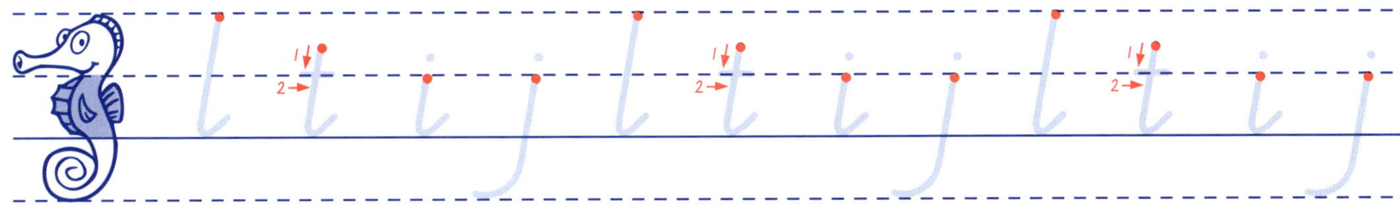

Trace, then copy.

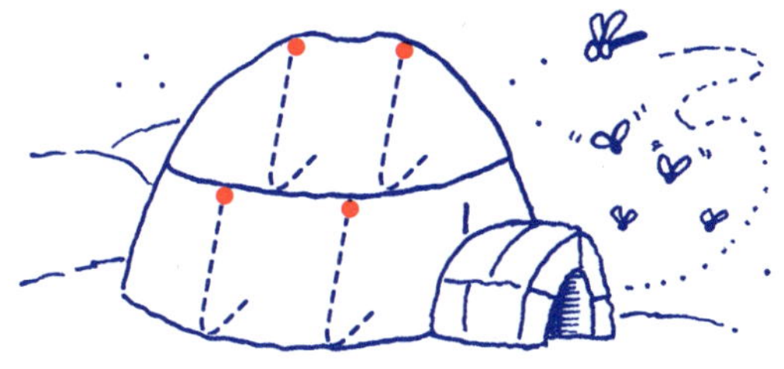

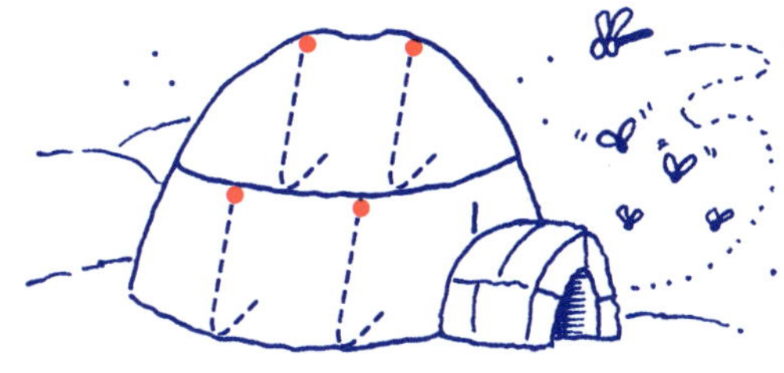

Colour the parts of the seahorse that show where the letter j sits.
Put a * on the tail of your best j and under your best J.

Find the j's.

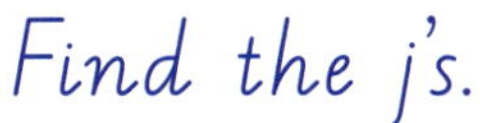

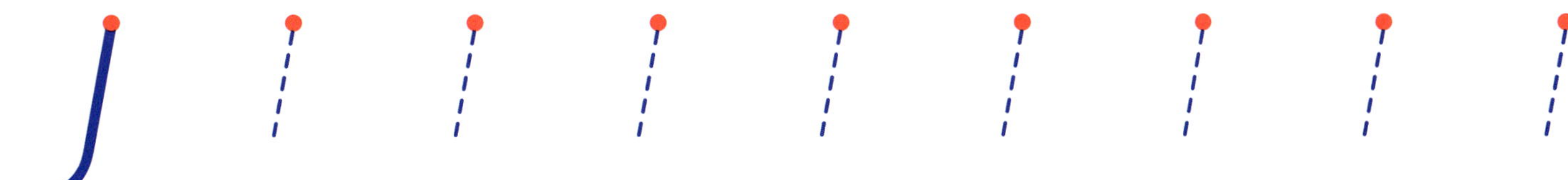

Trace the body and tail letters.

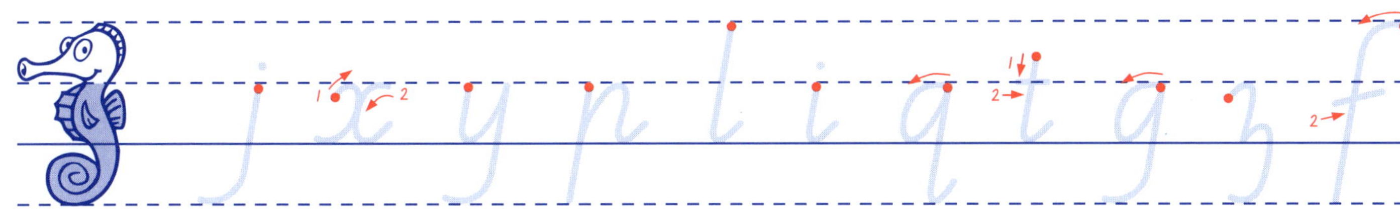

Trace, then copy. Don't forget to draw the seahorses.

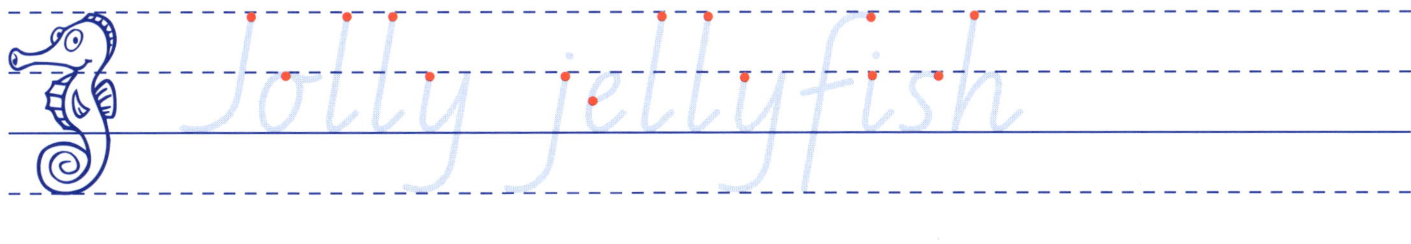

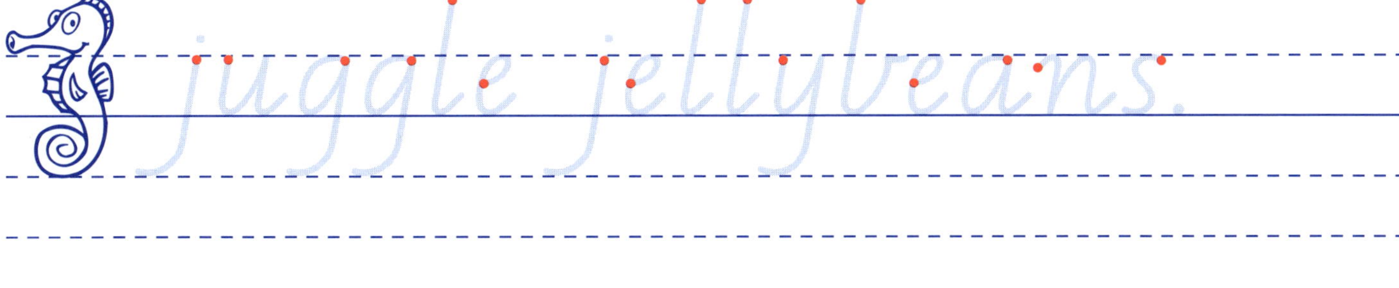

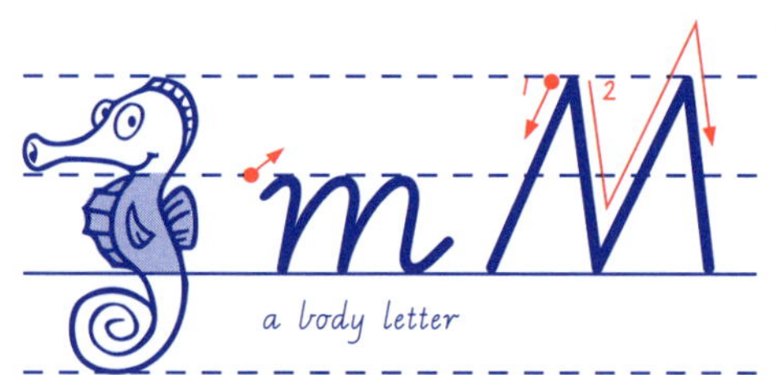

Track.

m m m m m m

Colour the parts of the seahorse that show where the letter m sits.
Put a ☐ around your best m and M.

m m m m m m

m

M M M M M

M

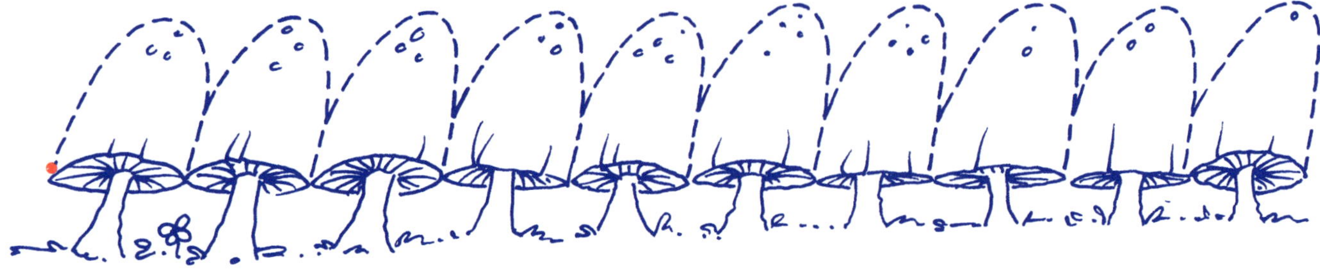

Find the m's.

m

Trace these clockwise letters. Colour the wedges in m, n and r.

m n r x z m n r

Trace, then copy.

Max Mouse loves

mangoes.

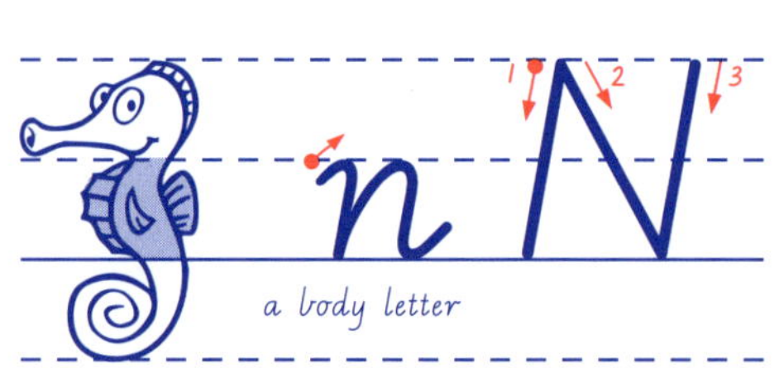

Track.

n n n n n n n

Colour the parts of the seahorse that show where the letter n sits.
Put a ✓ on your best n and N.

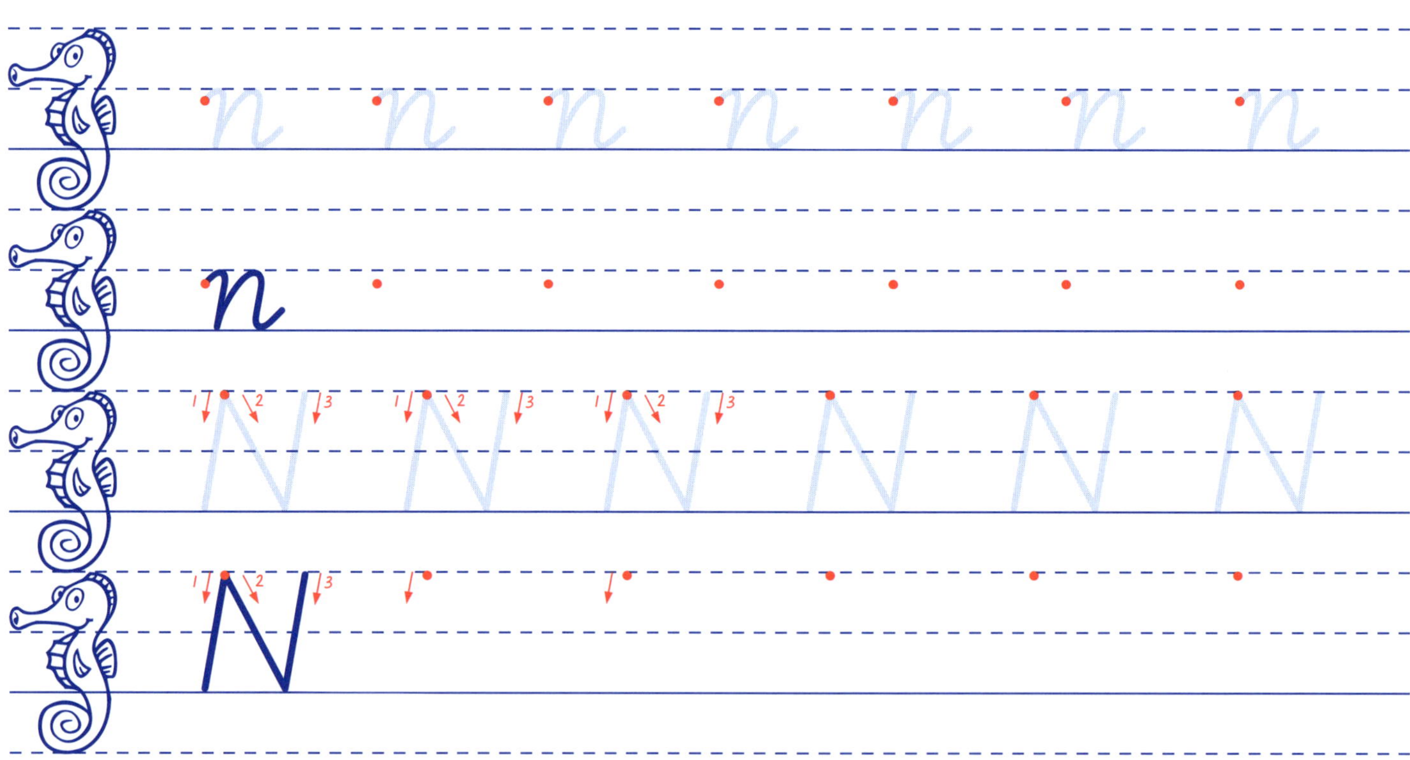

Find the n's.

n

Trace the body letters.

n m r x z n m r

Trace, then copy. Don't forget the full stop.

Nine numbats

are in the nest.

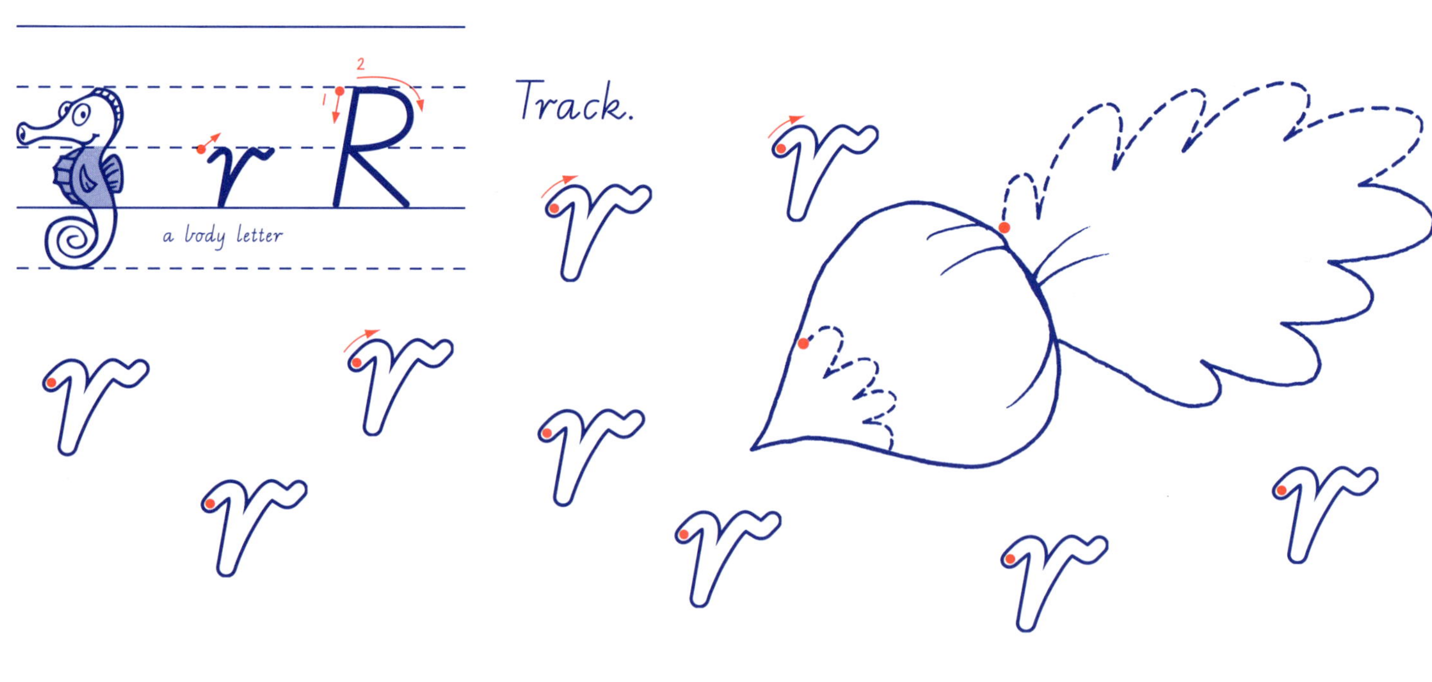

Colour the parts of the seahorse that show where the letter r sits.
Trace over your best r and R in red.

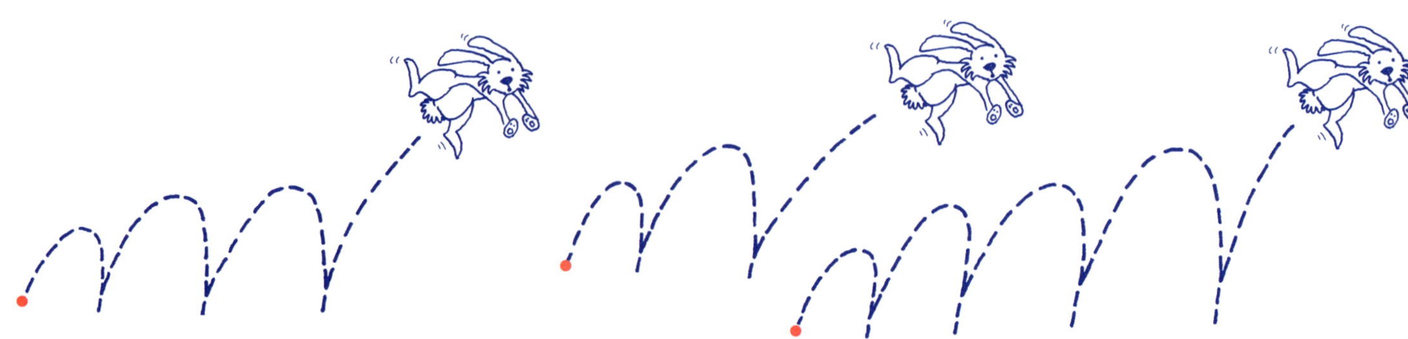

Find the r's.

Trace, then colour the wedges.

Trace, then copy. Circle the silent letter.

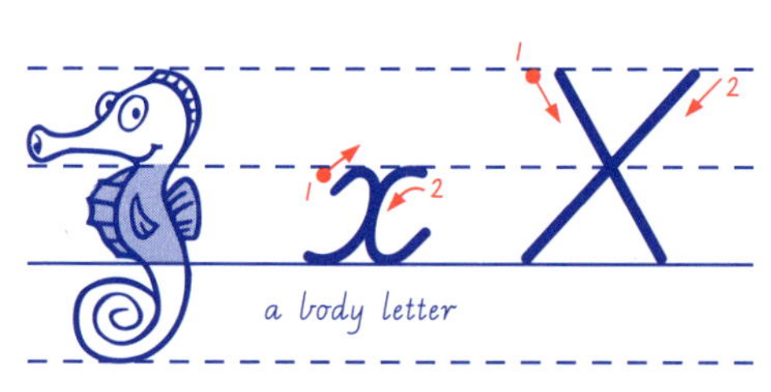

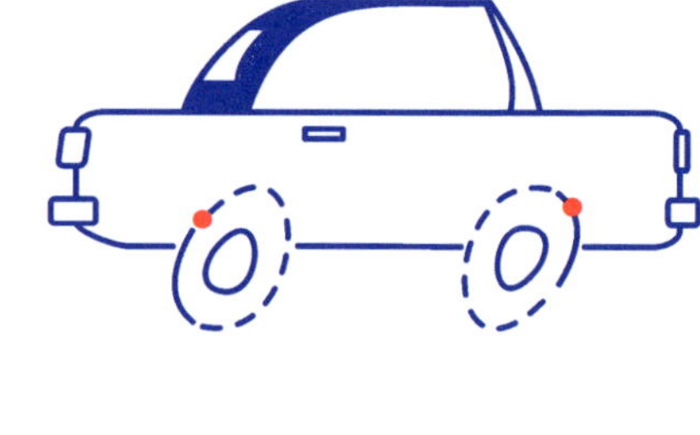

Track.

Colour the parts of the seahorse that show where the letter x sits.
Circle your best (x) and (X).

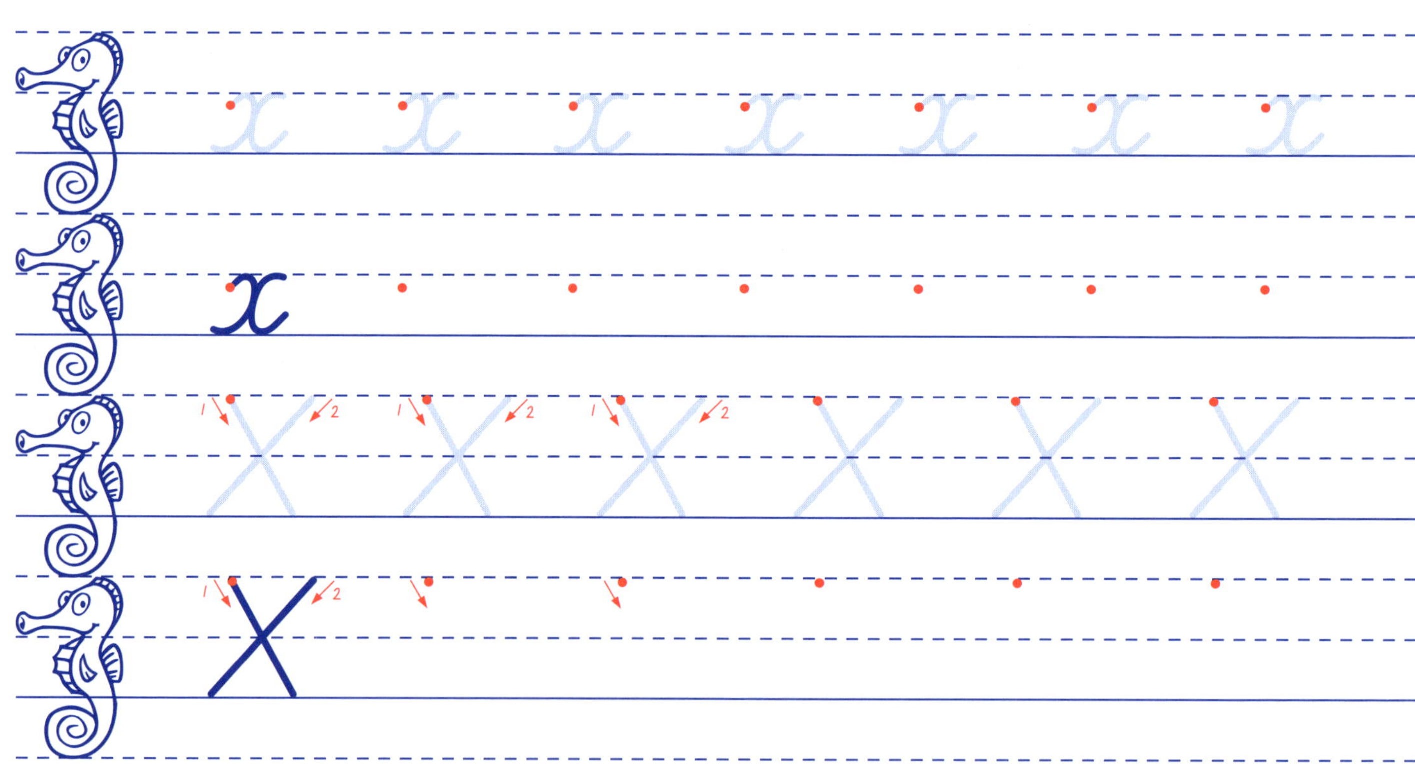

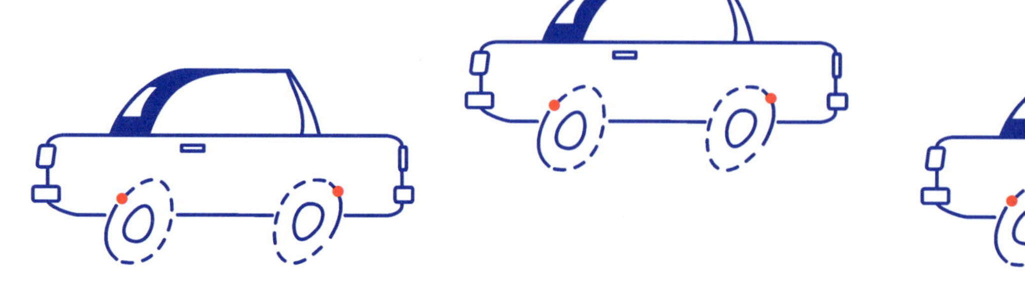

Find the x's.

Trace these clockwise letters.

r m n z x n m x

Trace, then copy. Don't forget to draw the seahorses.

Six foxes hide in

small boxes.

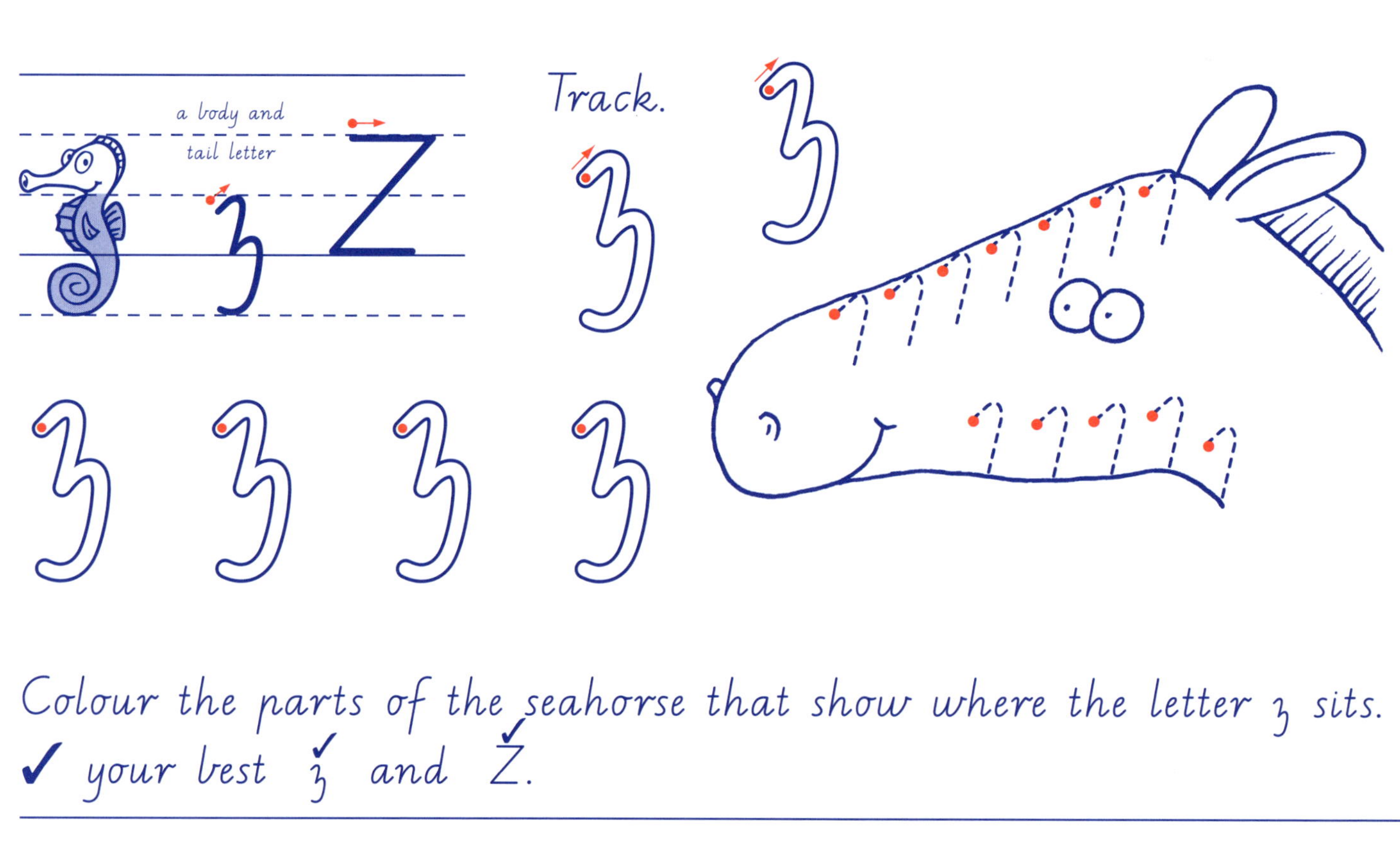

Colour the parts of the seahorse that show where the letter ʒ sits.
✓ your best ʒ and Z.

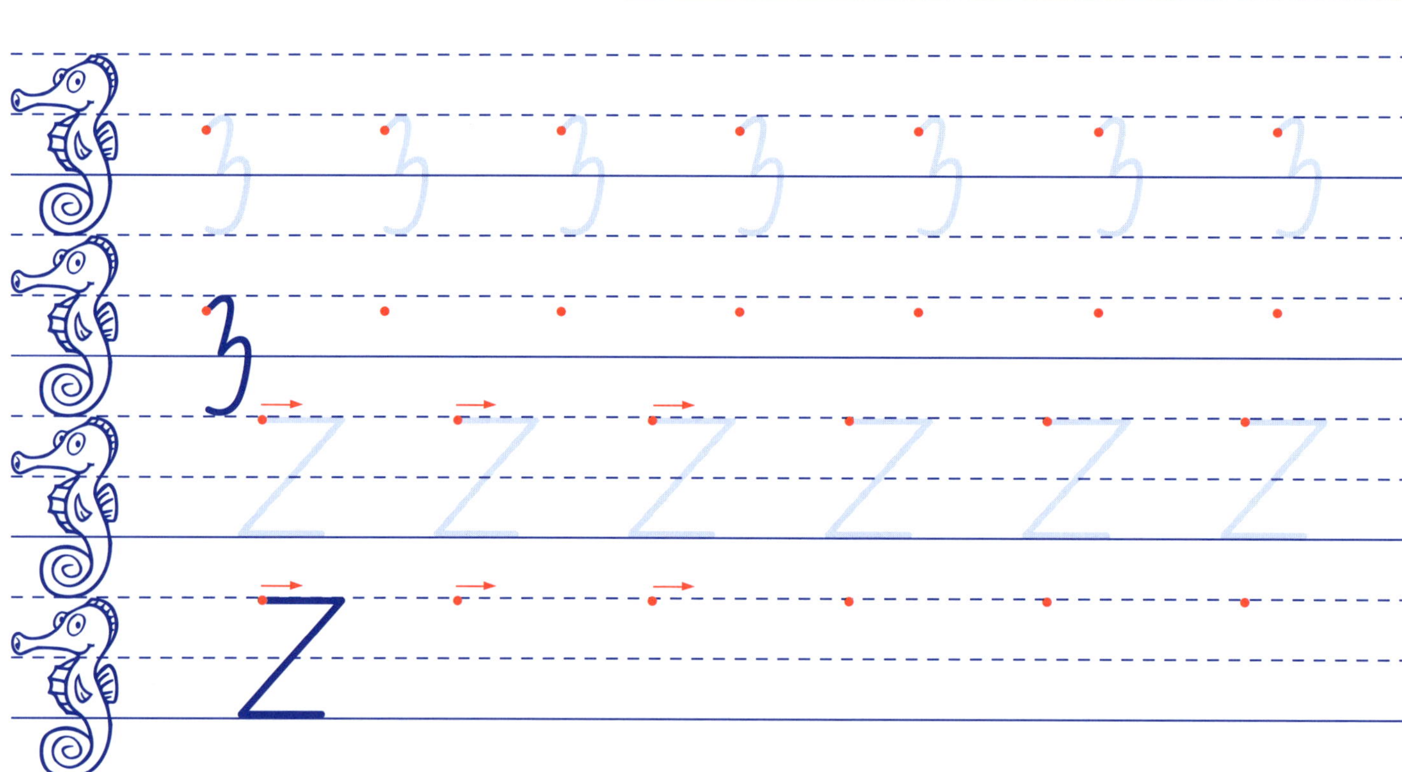

Trace.

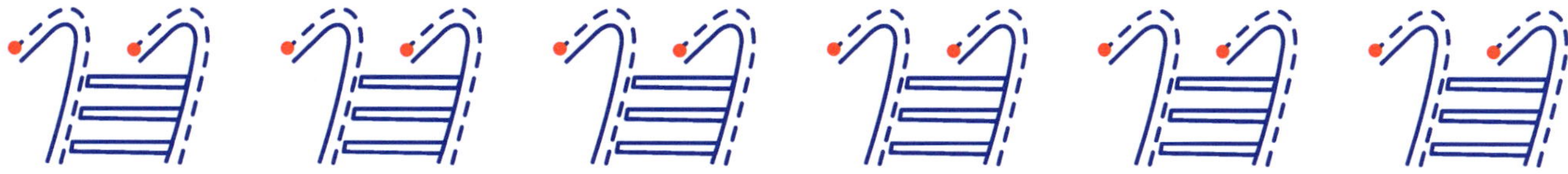

Trace the body letters.

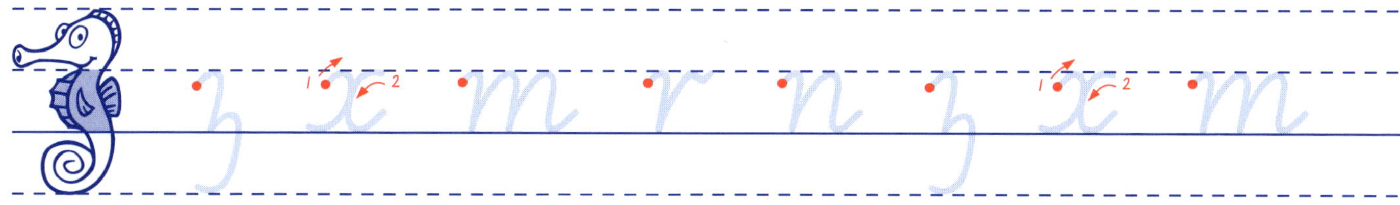

Trace, then copy. Don't forget the full stop.

a head and body letter
Track.
Colour the parts of the seahorse that show where the letter h sits.
Put a ❤ under your best h and H.
Left-handers

Find the h's.

Trace the head and body letters.

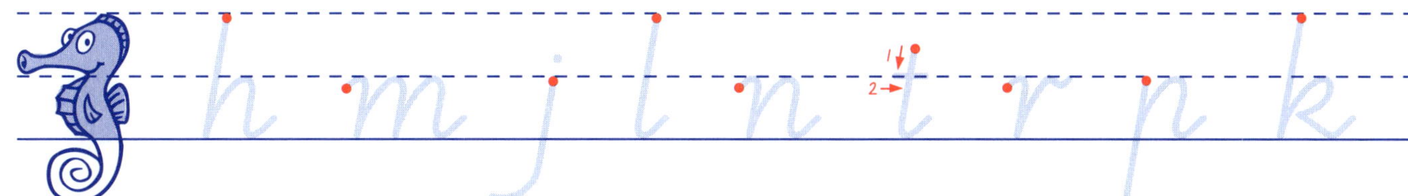

Trace, then copy. Don't forget to draw the seahorses.

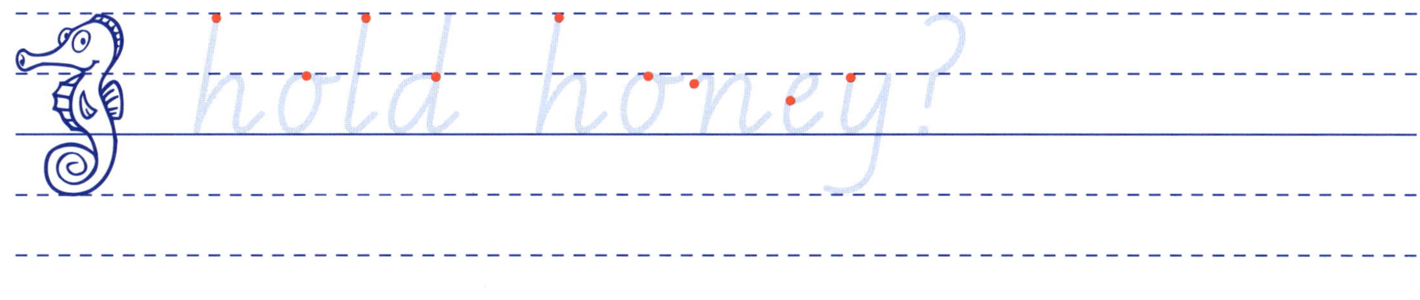

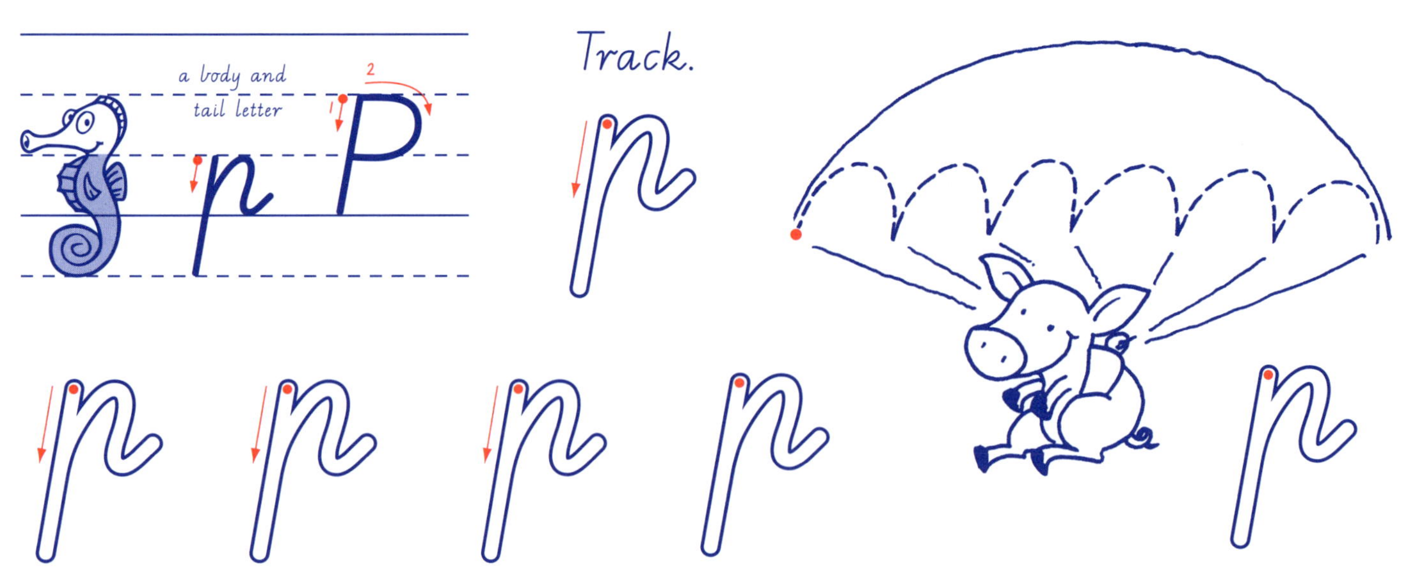

Colour the parts of the seahorse that show where the letter p sits.
Put a * in your best p and P.

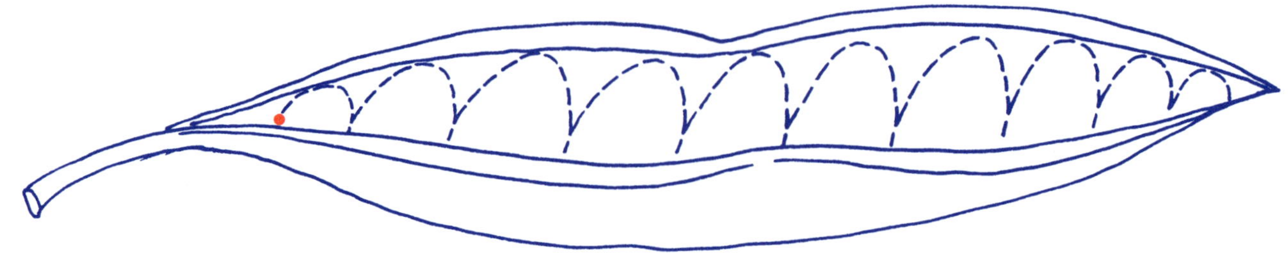

Find the p's.

Trace the body and tail letters.

p h y q r g b t j p

Trace, then copy. What is paisley?

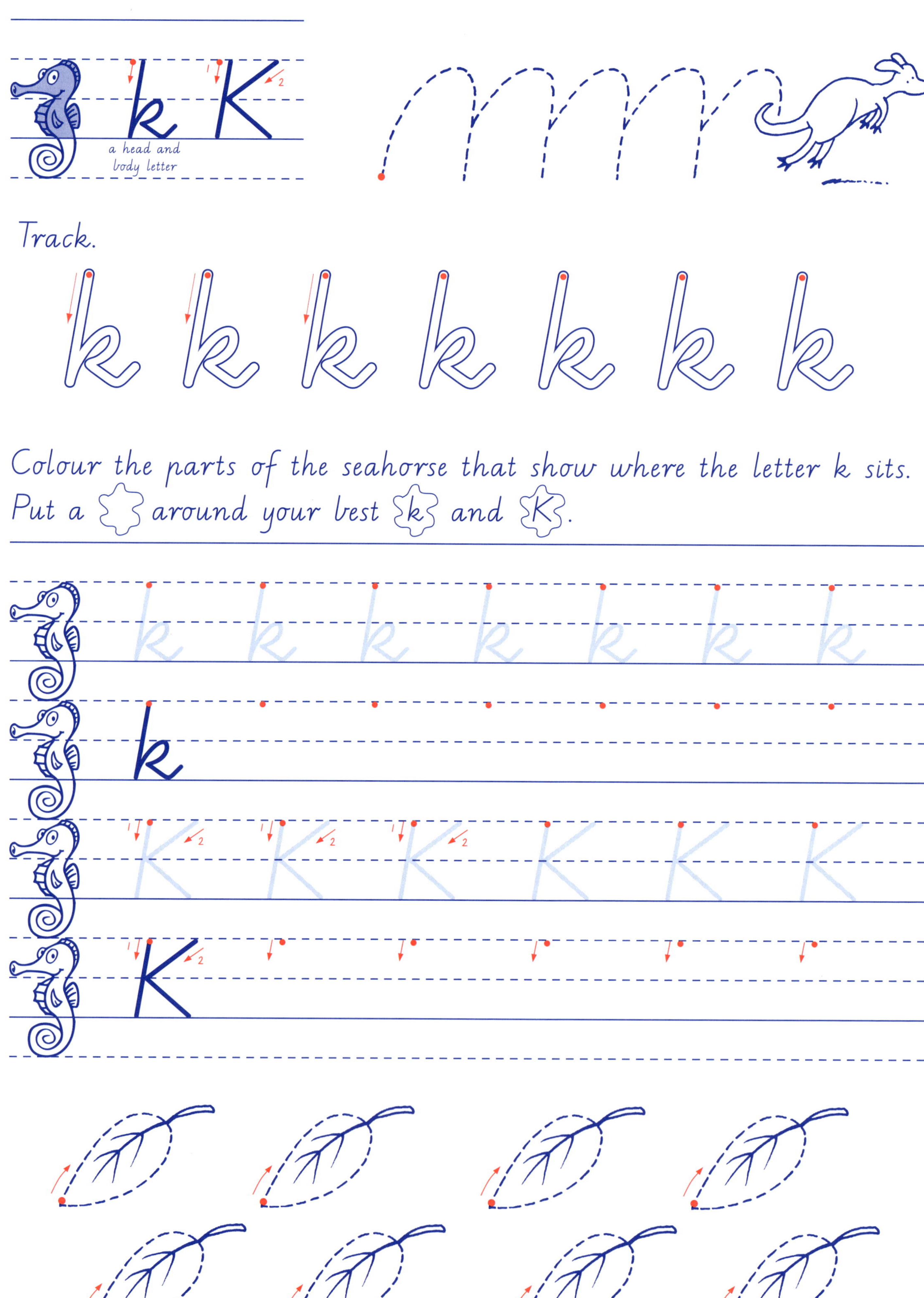
k K
a head and body letter
Track.
Colour the parts of the seahorse that show where the letter k sits.
Put a around your best k and K.

Find the k's.

Trace the clockwise letters.

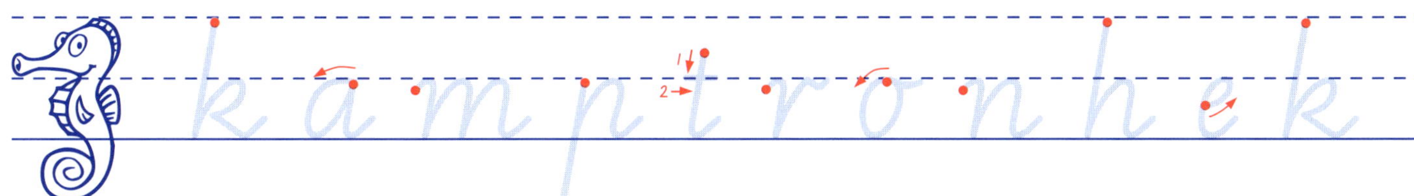

Trace, then copy.

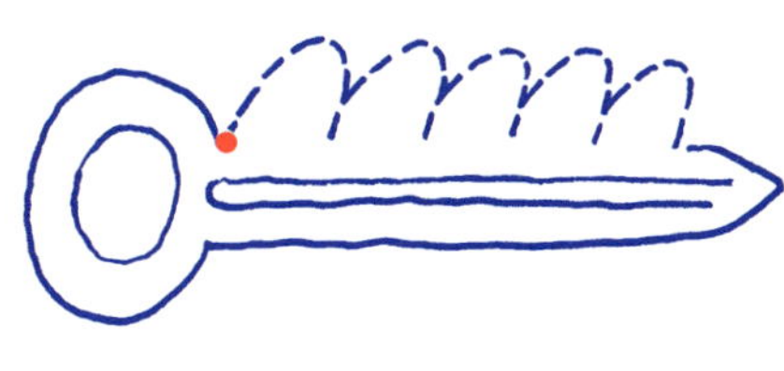

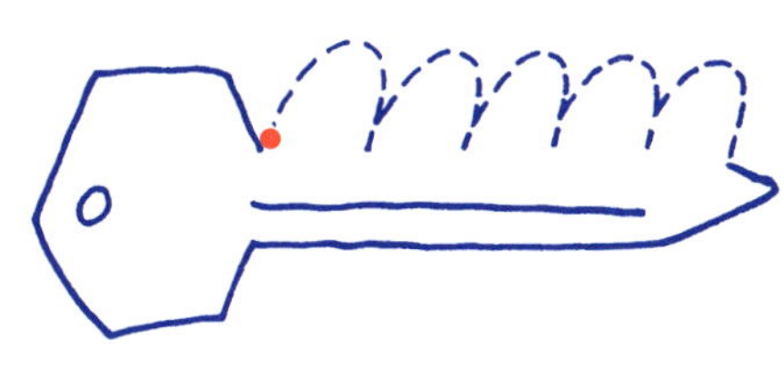

a A
a body letter
Track.
Colour the parts of the seahorse that show where the letter a sits.
Put an apple on top of your best a and A.
Left-handers

Find the a's.

Trace the anti-clockwise letters.

a c l t m d g q a c

Trace, then copy.

Angry ants ate

the apples.

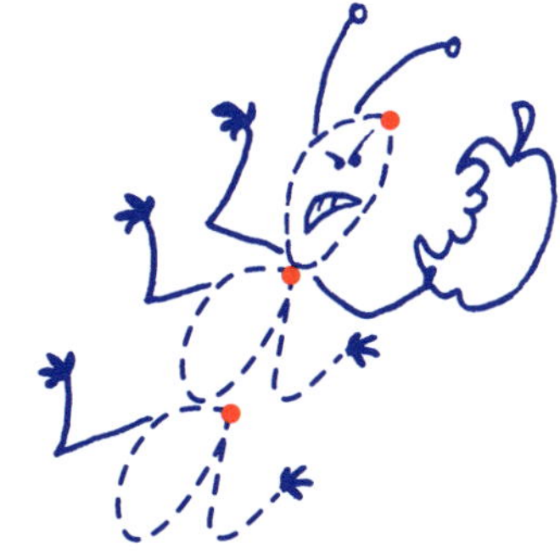

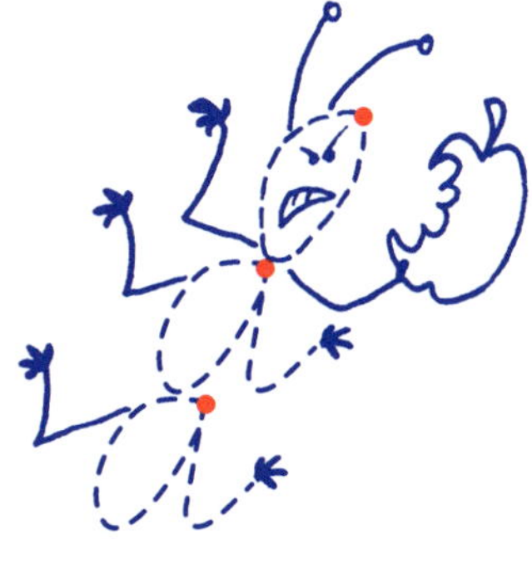

Colour the parts of the seahorse that show where the letter c sits.
Turn your best c and C into a 6.

Track.

Find the c's.

uc

Trace, then copy. Don't forget to draw the seahorses.

Coral cod hide

in coral caves.

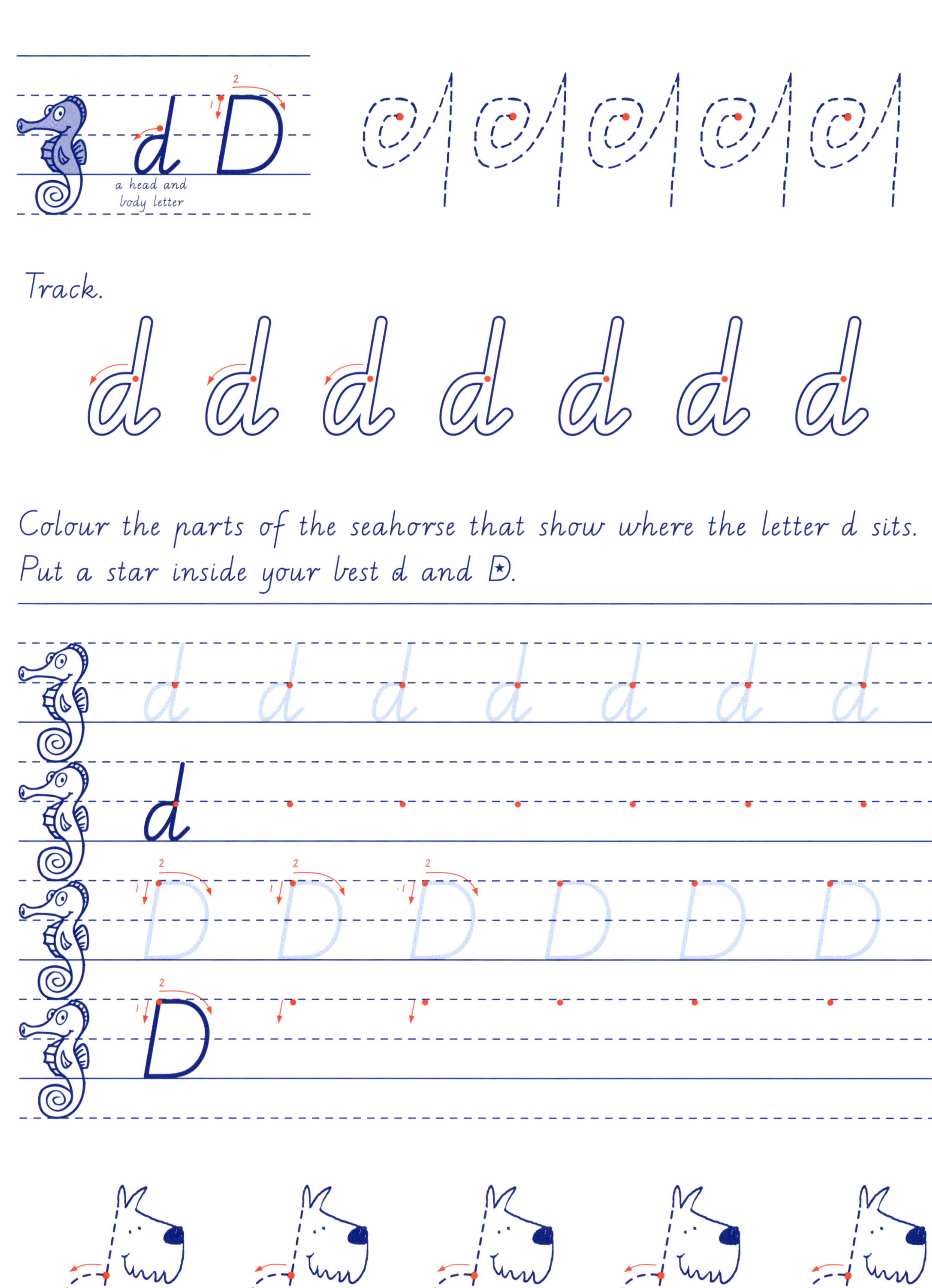

Track.

Colour the parts of the seahorse that show where the letter d sits.
Put a star inside your best d and D.

Find the d's.

Trace the head and body letters.

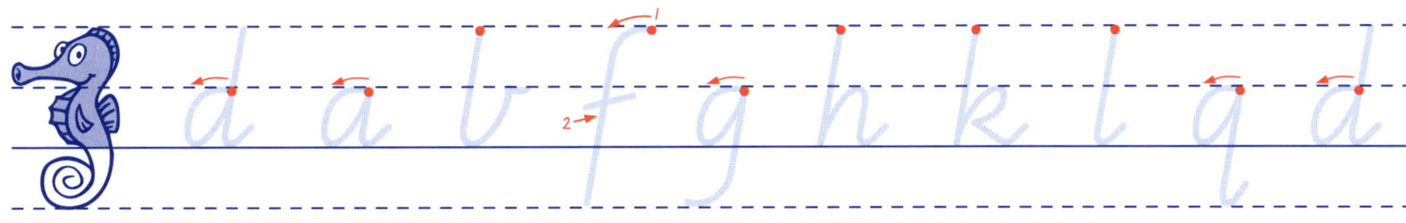

Trace, then copy. Colour in the wedges.

a body and tail letter
g G
g g
Track.
g g g g g
Colour the parts of the seahorse that show where the letter g sits.
✓ your best g and G.
g g g g g g g
g
G G G G G G
G

Find the g's.

Trace the anti-clockwise letters.

Trace, then copy.

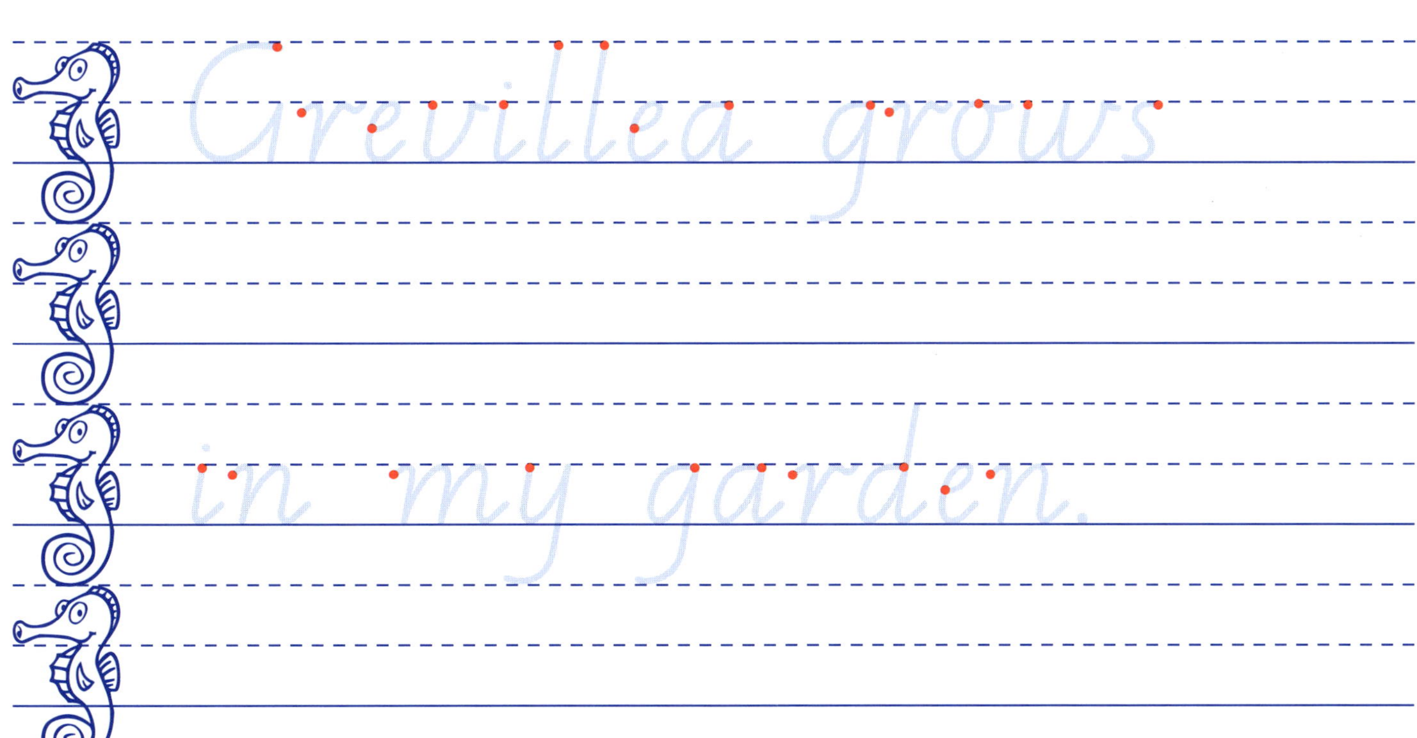

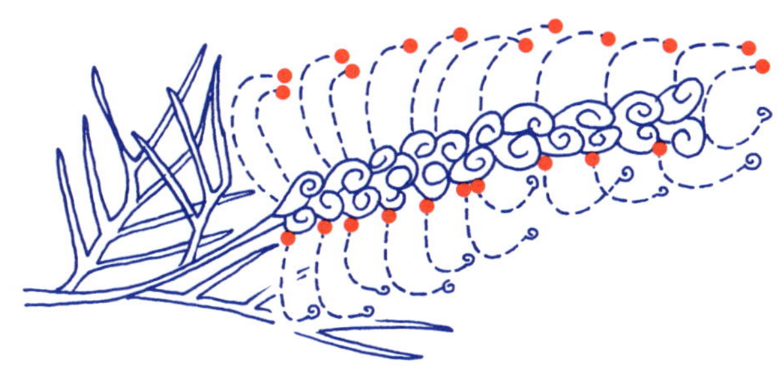

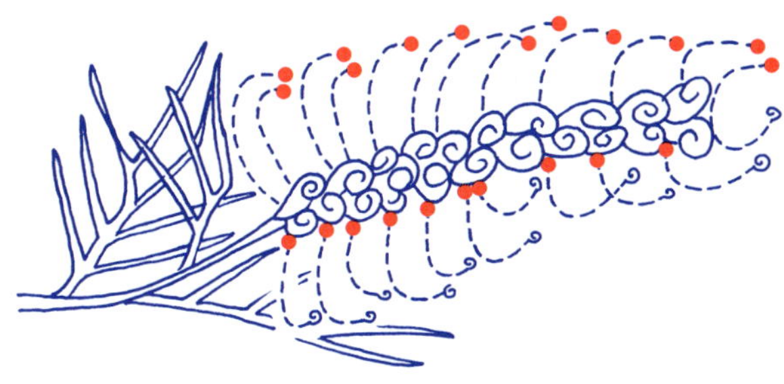

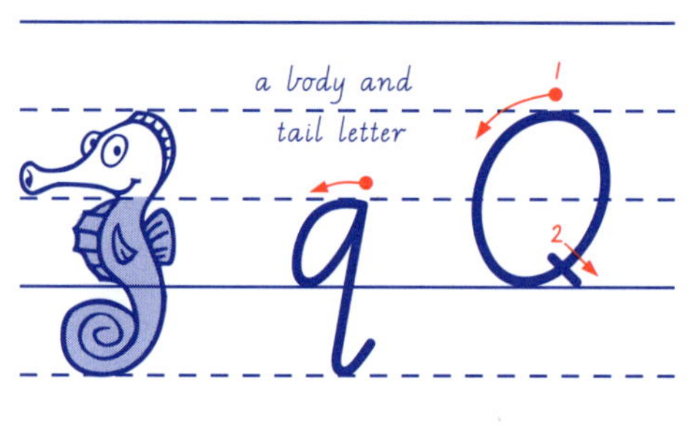

Track.

Colour the parts of the seahorse that show where the letter q sits.
Put a * on your best q and Q.

Find the q's.

Trace the q's. Colour the wedges.

Trace, then copy.

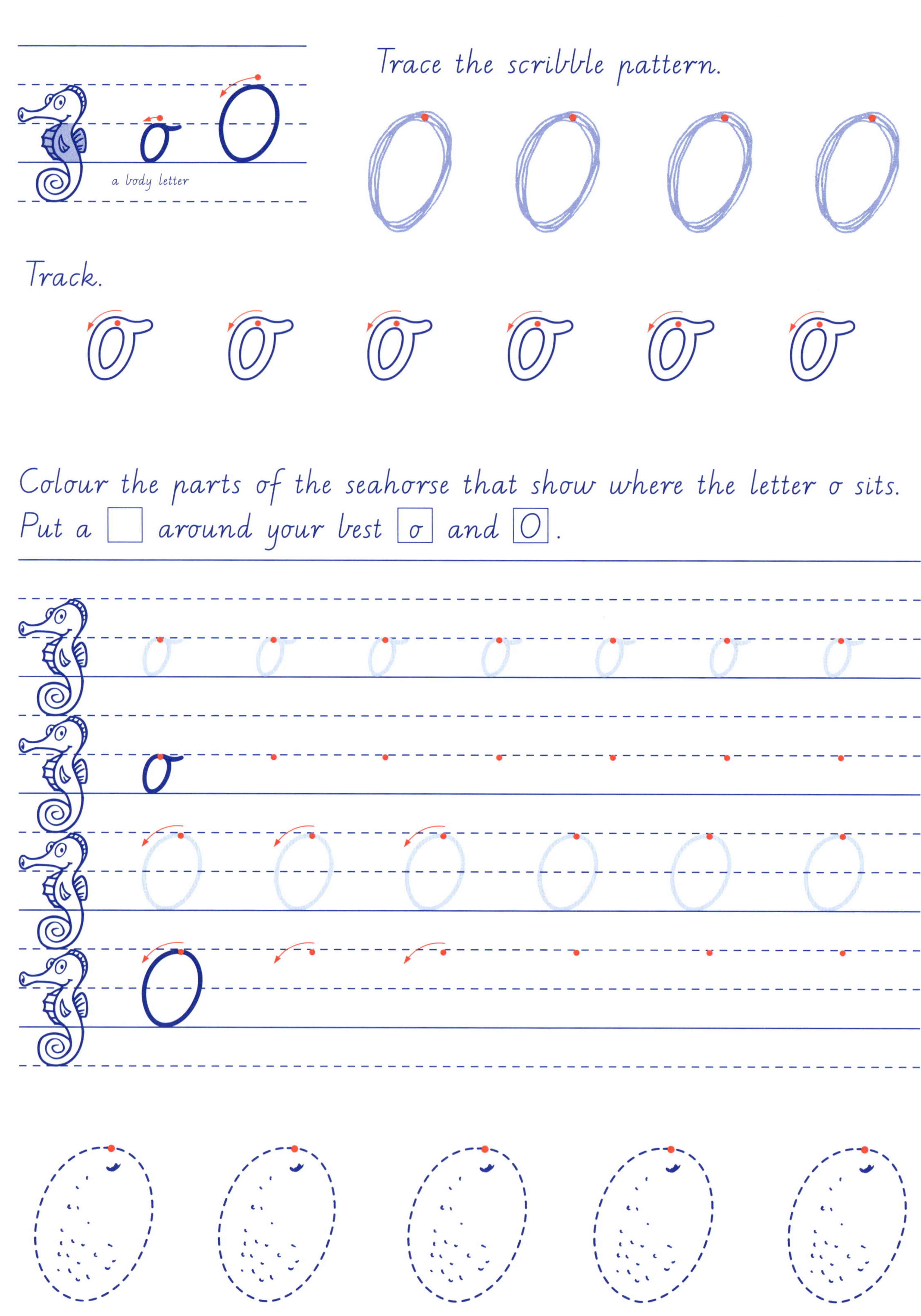

Trace the scribble pattern.

Track.

Colour the parts of the seahorse that show where the letter o sits.
Put a ☐ around your best o and O.

Find the o's.

Trace the body letters.

Trace, then copy. Underline the o's.

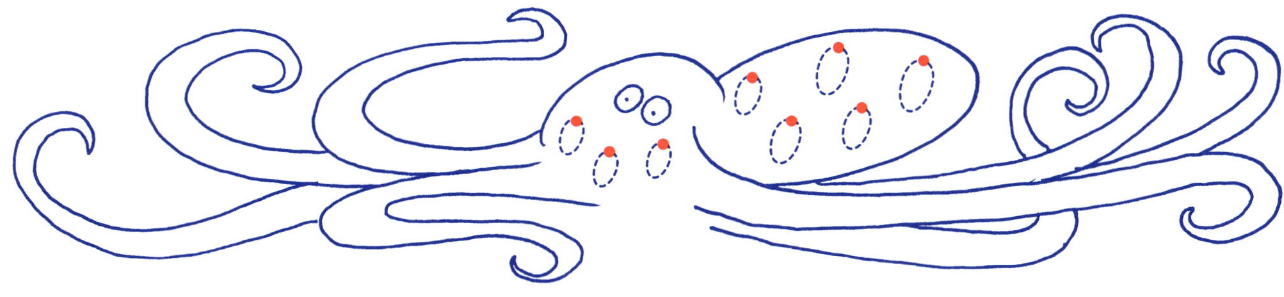

a body letter
Track.
Colour the parts of the seahorse that show where the letter e sits.
Put a ☐ around your best e and E.
Left-handers

Find the e's.

e

Trace, then copy. Underline the e's.

Eli sees three

green emu eggs.

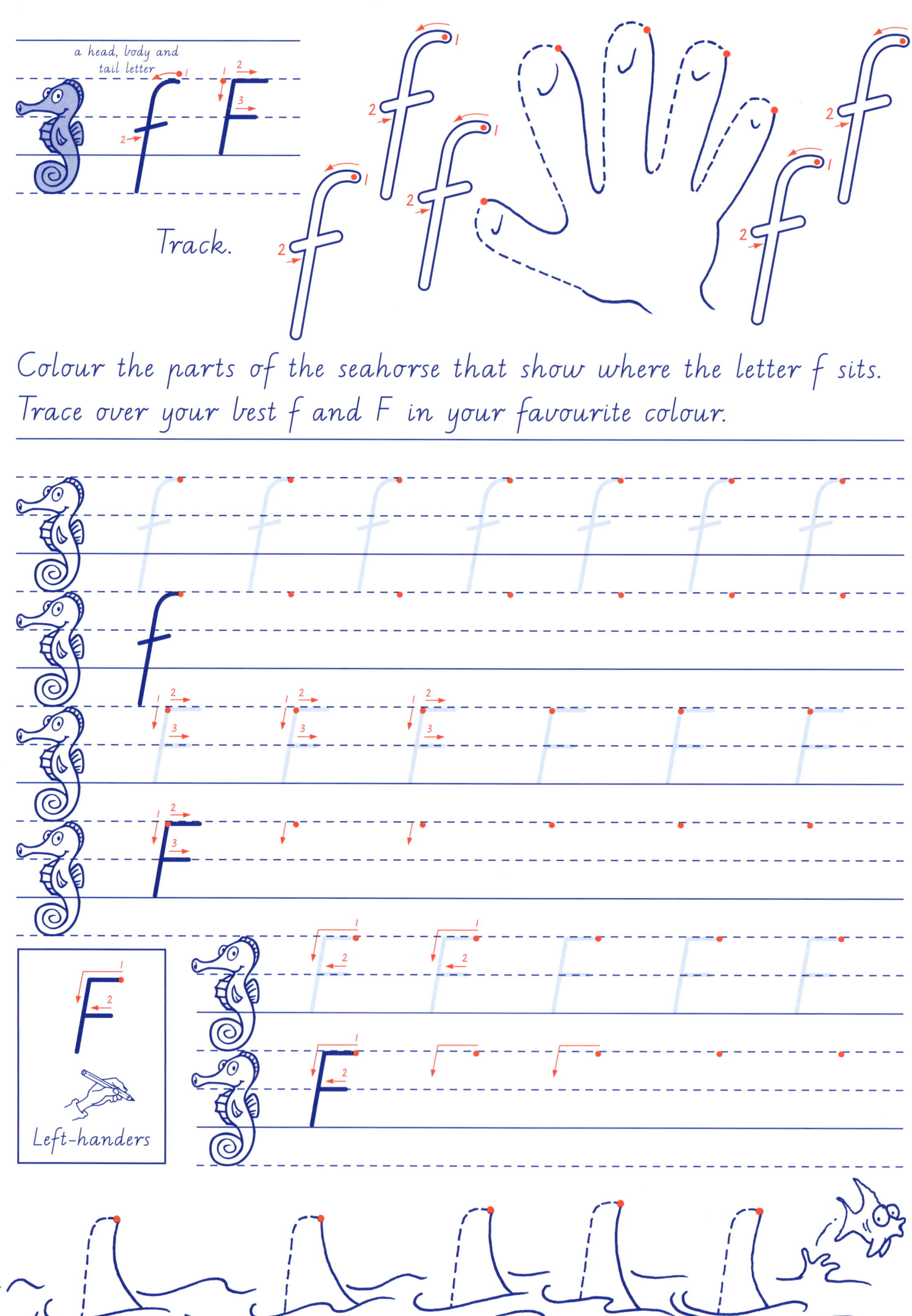

Colour the parts of the seahorse that show where the letter f sits.
Trace over your best f and F in your favourite colour.

Find the f's.

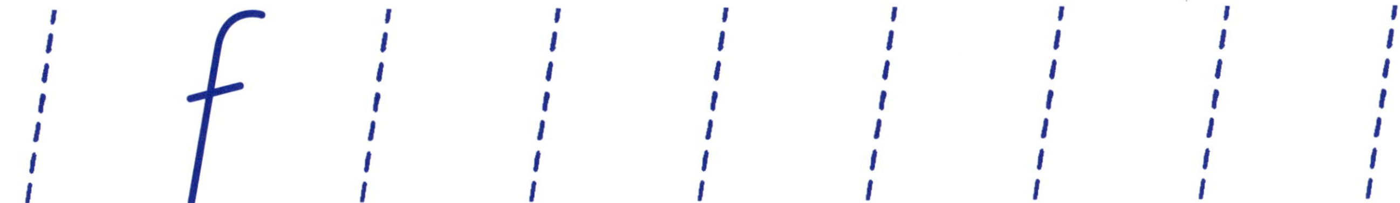

Trace the head and body letters.

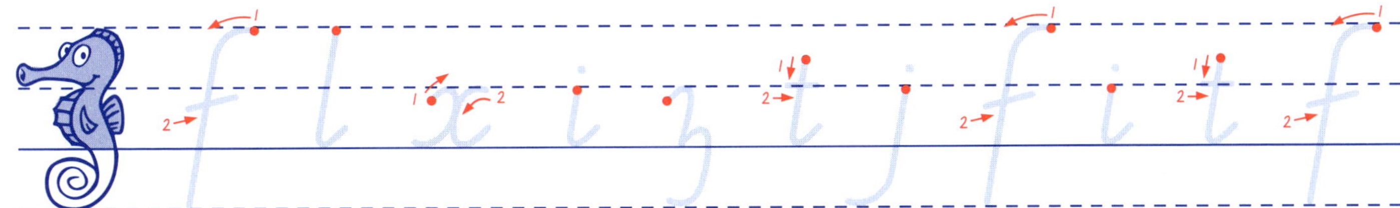

Trace, then copy. Put a line under any anti-clockwise letters.

s S
a body letter
Track.
Colour the parts of the seahorse that show where the letter s sits.
Turn your best s and S into a snake.
s
S

Find the s's.

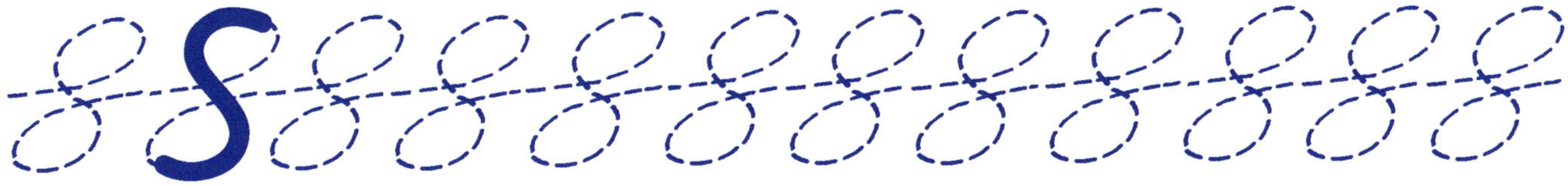

Trace the body letters.

s v e y u g w q c s

Trace, then copy.

Six sausages

sizzle and spit!

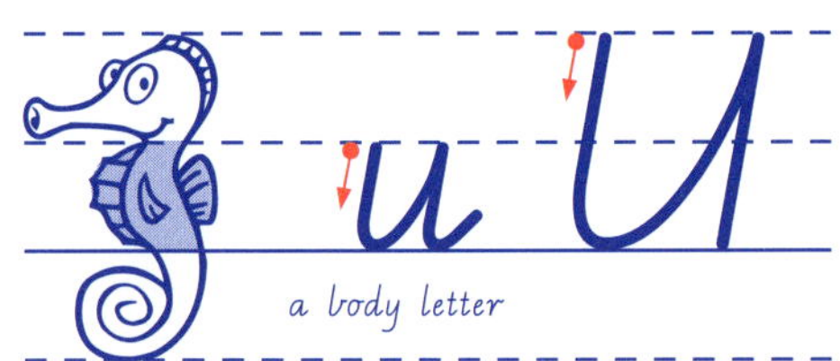

Track.

u u u u u u u

Colour the parts of the seahorse that show where the letter u sits.
Put a ✓ under your best u and U.

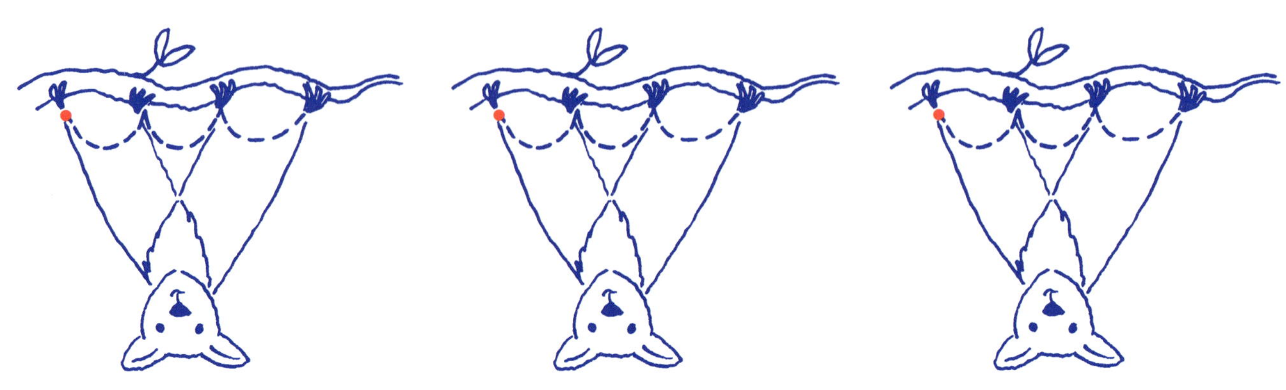

Find the u's.

u

Trace the pattern. Colour the wedges.

Trace, then copy.

Urchins use blue

umbrellas.

Colour the parts of the seahorse that show where the letter y sits.
Circle your best (y) and (Y).

Find the y's. Colour the wedges of cake.

Trace the body and tail letters.

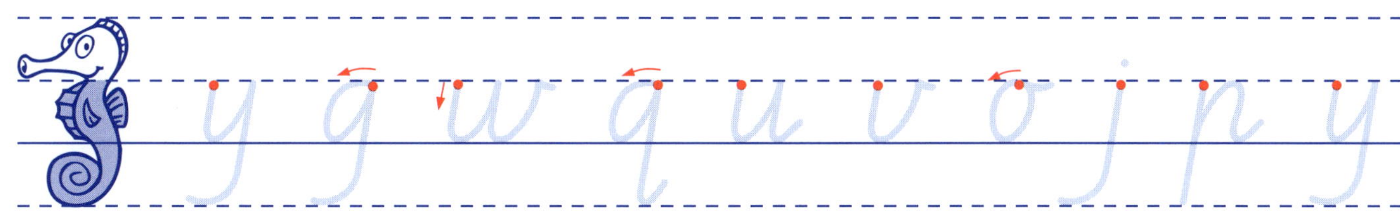

Trace, then copy.

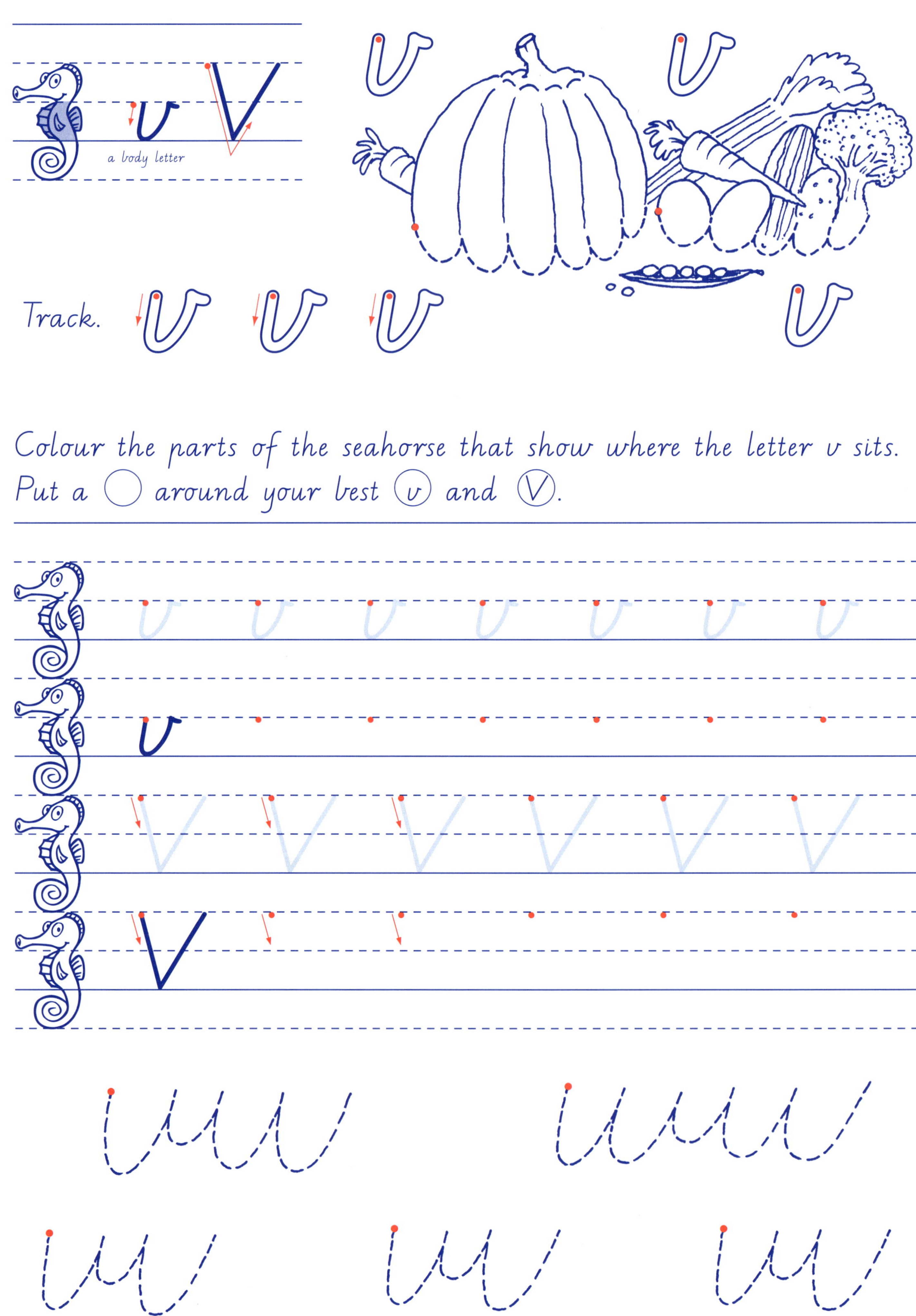

Colour the parts of the seahorse that show where the letter v sits.
Put a ◯ around your best ⓥ and Ⓥ.

Track.

Find the v's.

Trace, then copy. Underline the v's.

Five vases hold violets.

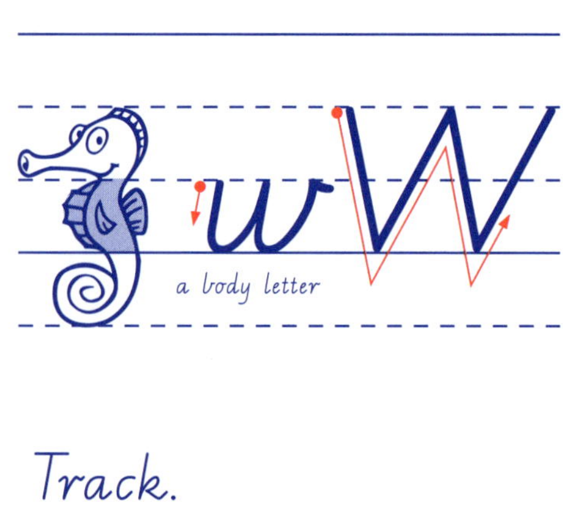

Track.

w w w w w w w

Colour the parts of the seahorse that show where the letter w sits.
Put a wiggle under your best w and W.

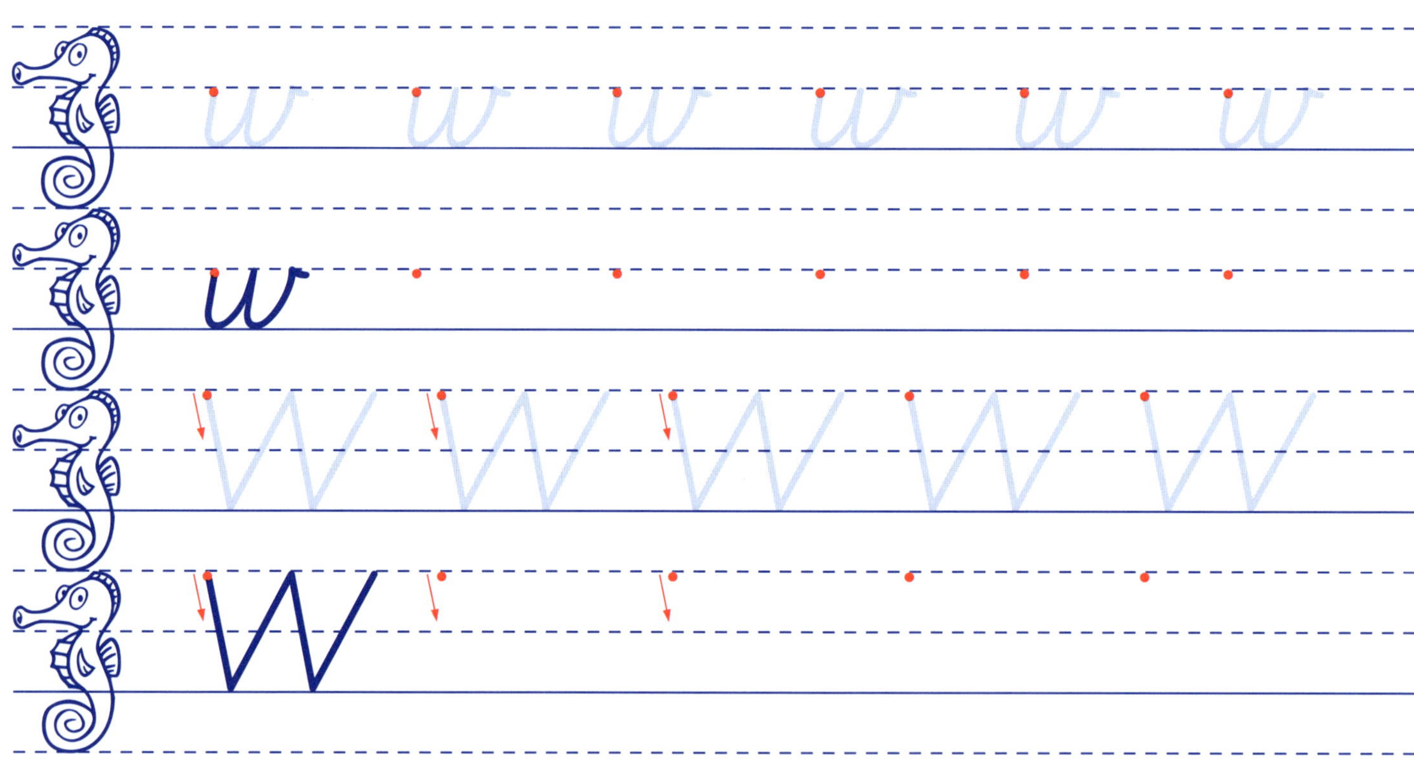

Find the w's.

Trace the body letters.

w d o u v g c a y w

Trace, then copy.

Wild winds

whip the waves!

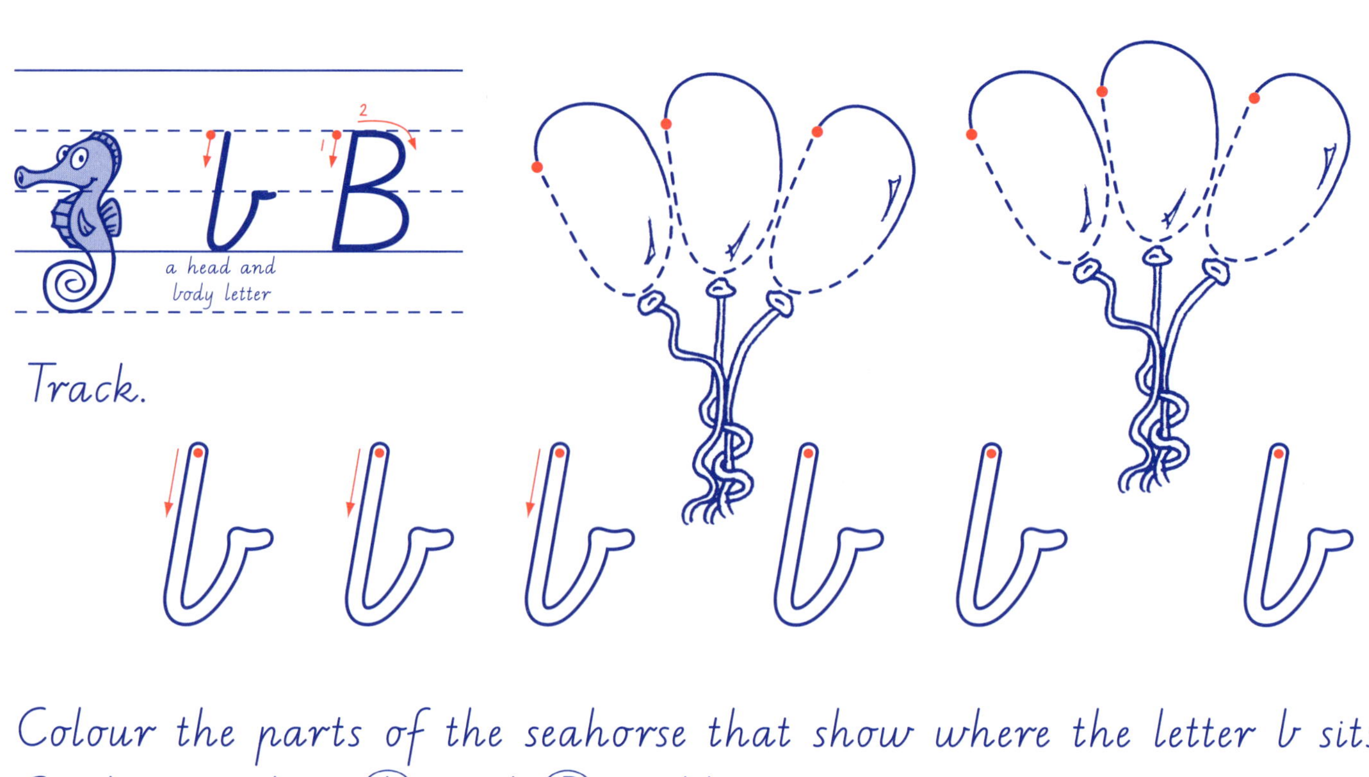

Colour the parts of the seahorse that show where the letter b sits.
Circle your best (b) and (B) in blue.

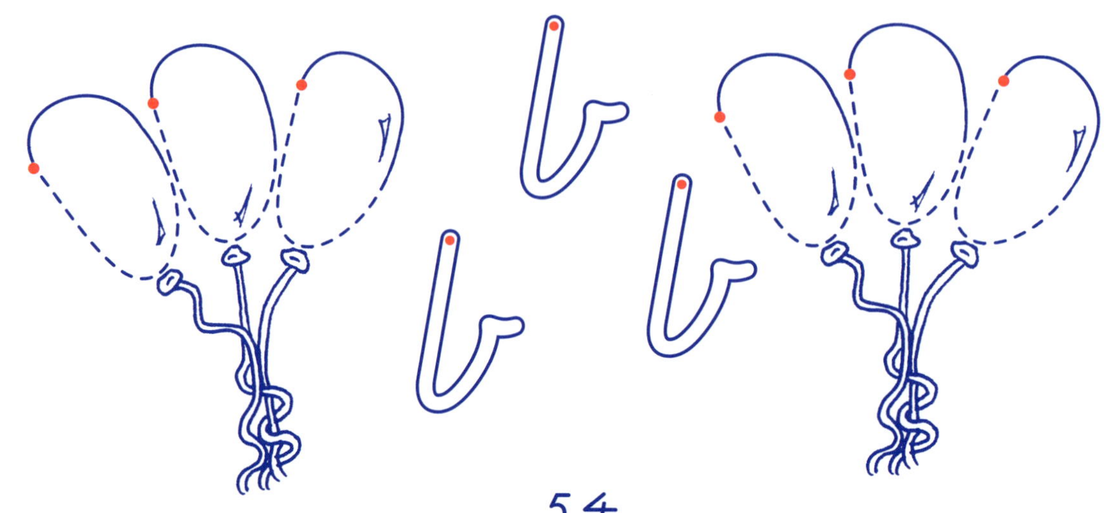

Track.

Find the b's.

ub

Trace, then copy. Circle the letters from the (u) famil(y) in (b)lue.

Baby Barney

bounces balls.

1 one

1 one

1 1 1

one

2 two

2 two

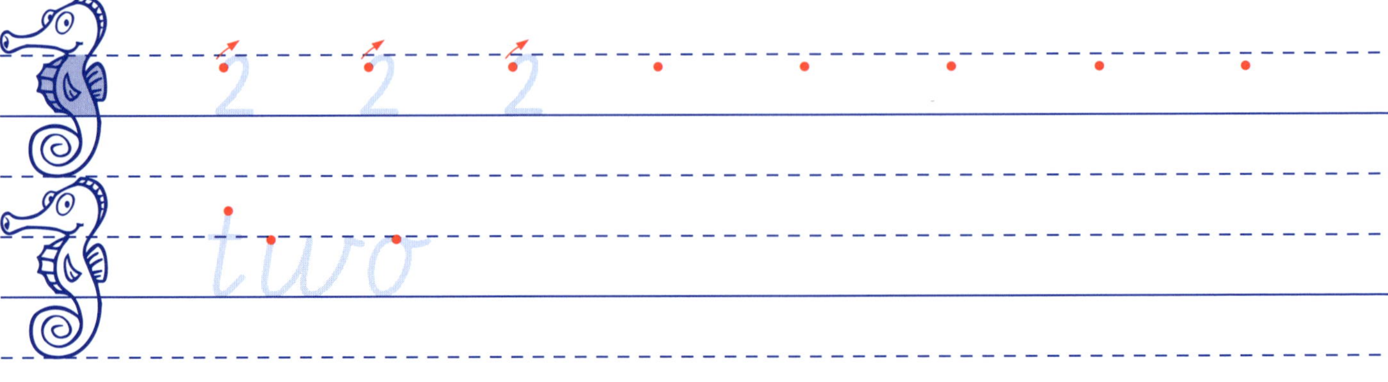

3 three 3 three

4 four 4 four

5 five 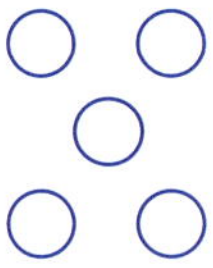 5 five

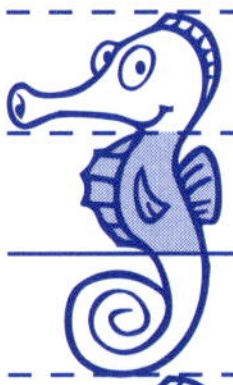
5 5 5

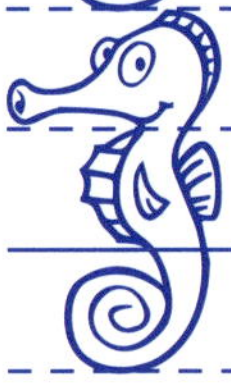
five

6 six 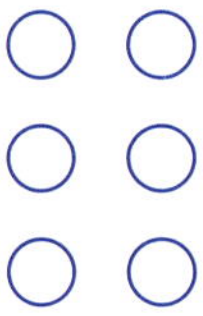 6 six

6 6 6

six

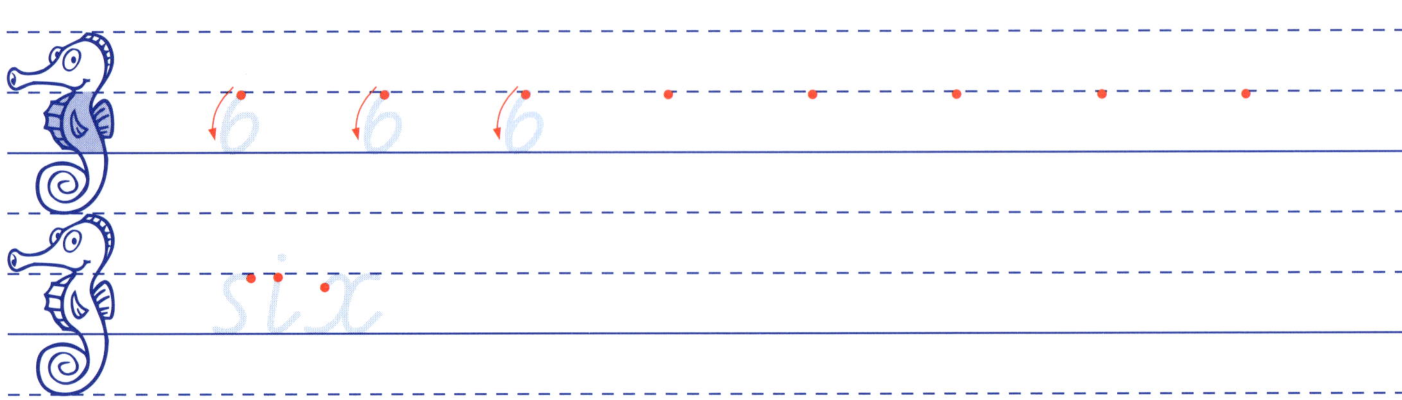

7 seven 7 seven

7 7 7

seven

8 eight 8 eight

8 8 8

eight

9 nine
9 nine
9 9 9
nine
10 ten
10 ten
10 10 10
ten

Trace, then write your own.

Trace, then write your own.

10

20

30

40

50

60

70

80

90

100